Building High Performance Agile Teams

by Made Tech

ISBN: 1544972687

First Printing: April 2017

www.madetech.com

Illustrations by Alexi McCarthy

Contents

Introduction

These days, software is becoming a huge part of increasingly more organisations and businesses. From content management systems to warehouse databases and e-commerce stores, software applications are fundamental to any successful business, yet frequently a source of frustration for the business owner.

Software teams are there to take that frustration away by creating software that provides a positive experience for both the organisation running it, and the audience using it. Whether in-house or external, the team responsible for building and maintaining that software needs to be well equipped to handle the challenges they'll face.

At Made Tech, our mission is to improve software delivery in every organisation we have the opportunity to work with and, with each organisation, we've spent a lot of time investigating how to build high performance, agile teams in order to produce the best software possible. This means taking stock of the day-to-day practices being used, both in the organisations we work with and our own, and looking at how they can be improved in such a way that the benefits are felt across the entire organisation.

This book breaks the subject down into three sections: Communication, Quality and Empowerment. Each section is composed of several essays written by the Made Tech team, previously published at www.madetech.com/blog.

Over the course of the next 15 chapters, you'll learn how you can build a great software team through practices such as making sure you have a communicative environment, giving the team ownership and responsibility of delivery, and allowing teams to structure the way they work.

Part 1: Communication

Delivering software well is hard. You need to master your language, framework and toolchain. You need to constantly refine processes to manage the flow of work. You need to stay on top of the constantly evolving technology landscape. But, more than this, you'll almost certainly need to work with others in some capacity.

While mastering the craft of software development is critical to delivering good software, a great many problems can be overcome with improved communication.

Creating an environment that values regular and open communication, both within the team delivering the product and with the wider stakeholder team, can go a long way to removing impediments in the delivery process.

In this first section of the book, we introduce strategies you can implement to promote a culture of communication and continuous introspection, ranging from pair programming to overhauling your feedback mechanisms.

CHAPTER 1

CREATING ENVIRONMENTS
THAT PROMOTE COMMUNICATION

In any organisation, one of the most powerful ways you can empower your team is to give them an environment that allows them to communicate freely at all levels. At Made Tech we actively encourage every member of the team to initiate or join any discussion that interests them, whether it be giving their opinion on how a part of the business runs, or introducing a new way of approaching how we work.

As a result, we've had valuable contributions from the entire team that have gone on to improve the way we work, build camaraderie and keep everyone up to speed on the goings on across the entire business.

The benefits of good communication

Visibility

As organisations grow, it's often easy for, as the saying goes, the left hand to have no idea what the right hand is doing. Project teams may not be aware of what each other is working on, it may not be clear to the wider team what pieces of work management are trying to win, and it's especially difficult for peers to know who is trying to develop a particular skill they might be able to help with.

As well as that, such a lack of visibility allows silos to develop naturally, where one or more developers wall themselves off to outside interference in order to concentrate on work. Whilst this is not a bad trait in moderation, left unchecked it can lead to those individual developers having exclusive domain knowledge, which then leads to bigger problems if there's a problem with the project they've been working on and they're unavailable for any reason.

By increasing visibility, via the methods described later in this chapter, teams gain a shared understanding of the direction the company is headed in, who's working on what, and individual projects. Team members are also actively able to help each other grow, which ultimately benefits the entire company.

Team cohesion

A good company culture is important, and giving your team ways to flex their tech muscles outside of obligations to customers is a great way to promote that. Whether it's an hour tackling a small, fun coding challenge, an entire day learning about a new technology, or a few days away on a company retreat, the time spent will go a long way to ensuring both that your team are getting exposure to technologies and practices that interest and excite them, and that they're becoming a stronger and more collaborative team for it.

Provide open channels to share knowledge

The first steps to creating a communicative environment for your team is establishing open forums in which everyone is invited to contribute as much as they'd like. We've got a few in place in Made Tech, all of which have had a positive impact on the way we work:

Continuous feedback

Continuous Feedback and its benefits are discussed at length in Chapter 7 but, in a nutshell: Continuous Feedback is the practice we use to encourage and address regular feedback from everyone, about everyone.

We found that annual reviews fell short in helping individuals learn and grow, and switching over to Continuous Feedback has allowed us to get a better sense of the goals people are trying to reach, and the areas in which they need improvement.

Importantly, it also allows us to act quickly to help them reach those goals, and give them the support they need in the areas in which they need improving.

Share progress and achievements with a weekly email

One of the problems we were having was that it often wasn't clear what other people outside of your team was working on week to week. They may have been on a new project, running with a new initiative, or on a recruiting drive. Our solution to this problem is what we've lovingly dubbed "TGIFs".

A TGIF is simply an email sent at the end of every Friday, with a short breakdown of what each of the various teams and departments within the company have achieved that week. Each team sends their breakdown to one person, and that person collates them all and sends out the email. TGIFs are a great way of giving your entire team visibility on what's happening within the company, and also reminding people of important events coming up the following week.

Comradrospectives

Retrospectives are a key component of the Agile process, occurring at the end of a period of work and allowing teams to reflect on what went well, what didn't go so well, and what they can learn from that.

We've re-appropriated that idea and applied it to the entire company, so that the entire team gathers together every few weeks to discuss our biggest sources of frustration, share our achievements, and figure out what we need to focus on in order to continue to improve the experience we provide to our customers, and the way we work.

Prior to each comradrospective, each team and department have a brief retrospective, and then bring the notes from that to the larger meeting. A Facilitator hosts the comradrospective, going around the room and prompting discussions about what each team found in their retrospectives. The Facilitator then looks for common threads between those discussions, which often leads to the highlighting of a wider company issue that can be focussed on over the next few weeks.

It should be noted that the role of Facilitator doesn't belong to one person, we actively encourage everyone on the team to take up the mantle for two reasons. One: each person will approach the role differently, ensuring comradrospectives never feel old, and two: it gives everyone a little bit of exposure to standing up in front of people and leading the conversation, which is valuable experience to have when your team is expected to present things like showcases to clients.

Presentations

No two individuals are alike, and within every organisation you're going to have an incredibly diverse set of interests and opinions. New technologies and frameworks are released to the public almost daily and, if your team are passionate about their craft, occasionally one of those technologies will resonate with someone on the team. They'll spend their own time researching it, decide whether it's for them and, if it is, spend even more time mastering it and becoming excited about the possibilities it provides.

As someone cultivating a communicative environment, it's important that everyone on your team knows they have a platform for sharing their excitement with everybody. Giving them the freedom to host presentations on topics they're enthusiastic about means everybody is regularly exposed to ideas and concepts that could potentially offer real value to your organisation.

This sort of exposure to new ideas and technologies then leads to a willingness to implement them in future projects, meaning your organisation is constantly evolving, rather than sticking with practices that will ultimately end up outmoded or obsolete.

Hack days

Hack days are another great way of exposing your team to new technologies. They're also a way to mix things up and potentially even produce products you or your customers will use for a long time.

As an example, a customer of ours wasn't aware of that their SSL certificate was due to expire, leading to browsers designating their website as insecure. This is a problem we've seen in organisations as big as Instagram, so we decided to hold a hack day dedicated to solving the problem.

The result was SSLCatch, a relatively small application that simply alerts domain owners in the days, weeks and months before an SSL certificate is due to expire. The whole team worked together over eight hours, regularly communicating with each other to get the clearest sense of what everybody was working on, solve blocking issues and ultimately get the application live as quickly as possible.

We now have hack days every one to two months, and they've often resulted in new internal tools we use regularly. More than that, they're always a great opportunity to get the whole team swarming on a single project, solving problems together.

Regular standups

Daily standups, also known as scrum meetings, are an important tool for getting everyone up to speed on what people will be working on that day. Teams can highlight any issues they have, or how they can help others facing their own issues.

Daily standups should be short, around ten minutes max, and should only involve team members working on the same project or in the same department.

Extreme Programming

Extreme programming is a popular methodology that encompasses many different programming practices, most of which are beyond the scope of this article. That said, two practices in particular are very useful when it comes to promoting communication within your team: pair programming and "whole team".

Pair programming

We'll discuss pair programming in Chapter 4 but, in short, pair programming leads to stronger communication by encouraging each programmer to articulate their thought processes and engage in conversation about the best possible solution for the problem they're facing.

Whole team

The phrase "whole team" refers to a way of working in which teams are given the freedom to organise themselves, and whose team members can, between them and their various sets of skills, can solve any technical challenge a project might present.

As well as that, when building software for

customers, one of the biggest sources of frustration is often not being able to get hold of the customer when a critical question about the work arises. "Whole team" then, means having the customer, at the beginning of the engagement, designate one of their own team to be the Product Owner throughout.

The role of the Product Owner is to be available at all times to your team, so that they can give guidance and answers to your team as and when they need it. In our experience with Product Owners, we've found that having the Product Owner on site leads to an even better experience, as they're instantly more approachable and, from a wider business perspective, it becomes very easy to build a relationship with the customer.

Challenges in maintaining good communication

Tuning out

Every programmer knows the feeling of being in flow, when they're highly focussed and incredibly productive. It's very important not to make that state harder to achieve, as it can lead to frustration. Even so, left unchecked, it can be tempting for some to almost permanently block everything else out, forging ahead on their own path and rarely communicating with the rest of their team.

This then leads to either the programmer having exclusive domain knowledge over a significant part of the application and becoming a silo, or spending time going down a path of work without getting more information from others, potentially producing something that can't be used.

Too many cooks

On the flip side, too much communication is A Bad Thing. Making time to communicate is important, but when it comes down to it you need to make sure the work you're communicating about is getting done. Pushing communication too much can lead to discussions or debates where there are too many opinions, and finding an actionable outcome to them proves impossible and time consuming.

While it's important to make sure everyone has a voice within your organisation, there will inevitably be times when action needs to be taken, but you're debilitated by too much discussion. Judge these situations carefully, and don't be afraid to take the lead if it means resolving a conversation that's gone on for too long.

By giving your team an environment in which they're able to communicate freely about whatever excites them, challenges they're facing, how your team could be doing things differently and ways they can help each other improve, you're ensuring your organisation is able to constantly grow and meet any challenge an ever changing industry throws at you.

by Scott Mason

CHAPTER 2
AGILE PLANNING

Both words, "agile" and "planning", mean different things to different people. In this chapter I hope to provide an overview of agile planning without going into specific implementations like Scrum or Kanban whilst still providing practical advice for any implementation.

For the purpose of this chapter, agile planning refers to the organisation of teams and work in order to deliver value iteratively. You might consider it a strategy where planning is not a phase and is not completed ahead of implementation but instead happens frequently during a delivery, enabling teams to adapt to change.

Start with the value

Every project will want to provide value to an organisation or person. If we choose agile we may not plan and document everything up front but we'll always be working towards a known, or partially known, value. It makes sense then to understand the shapes that value can take and work out what high level value we want to achieve.

We can group our value into 5 abstractions. Each deal with a different unit, each with their own stakeholders to whom they provide value.

- **Vision** is the central mass that holds the project together

- **Goals** are quantifiable measurements of value

- **Capabilities** are provided in order to reach goals

- **Features** implement capabilities

- **Tasks** are the units of work that produce features

You can read more about these units in Liz Keogh's article on estimating complexity[1]. She first introduced me to this idea and it's stuck with me ever since.

Even if you haven't knowingly defined these units before, your project will likely have them. They are natural artifacts of software engineering projects. Your team may not be aware of the vision, but your product owner or the manager ensuring the project's completion should do. Your team may be asked to complete a set of features without being given the freedom to consider alternative ways of providing capabilities. Start with a vision and goals that work towards it.

I hope those reading this chapter, those that haven't always identified vision and goals, capabilities and features, will be able to identify them in future. Even better, have the team understand and help define them. If you do not have a vision and set of related goals defined for your product or project, grab your team and stakeholders and define them now.

Layers of agile delivery

You could see the project's vision, goals, capabilities, features and tasks each as interdependent layers. Each layer helps achieve the layer above them. Goals implement a vision, capabilities implement goals, features capabilities and so on. This is the direction of the dependence.

---

1   https://lizkeogh.com/2014/06/06/goals-vs-capabilities/

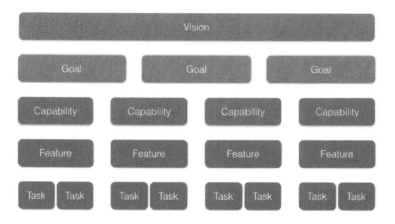

Never assume a feature is the only way to provide a capability. When you think about each layer's dependencies as travelling in a single direction, as a single direction of authority, you begin to think less in solutions and more in problems. You start with a vision, this is the highest authority. Your vision defines its goals. Goals then require capabilities. Only then do our capabilities need features to implement them. Why then do we march into new projects with a bunch of features in our heads? Probably because they're the most tangible output of a project but that doesn't make it sensible, or agile at that.

A charity might have a vision to provide free access to travel for the elderly. A goal to measure the success of this vision might be to provide 10 elderly people free access to travel a week. Now, in order to provide 10 elderly people free access to travel, we'll need a way of transporting them.

Transportation is our capability. Only then do we consider a feature that provides this capability. We might choose taxi, bus, volunteer driver, spaceship or a mixture of them. The point is we haven't locked ourselves to a particular solution. We've left our options open.

When features become subservient to our capabilities, goals and vision we are no longer so attached them them. When we realise a feature is going to take too long to deliver we can consider our alternatives. When a goal needs to change, we are more inclined to let go of the capabilities and features as we know the success of our project is related to it's goals and not how those goals are implemented.

Moving through the layers with iterations

Agile teams will use iterations to complete tasks. They might have several iterations for one task, or complete many tasks in a single iteration. What is common is the use of an iteration to receive feedback on work completed to ensure it's meeting expectations and providing value. Iterations enable us to move down through the layers understanding the problem all the way down to individual tasks, and then we travel all the way back up solving problems at each abstraction.

Be clear on your purpose, bring it back to the vision. During an iteration we travel through each layer in order to understand the problem. In order to decide on a feature we must understand what capability we are trying to provide, the vision and goals can help us make decisions.

We might only track tasks on our board and capabilities on our roadmap but it's always useful to keep the parent abstractions in mind. Write up your vision and goals above your boards and maps. At the beginning of every stand up, reiterate the feature you're working towards before describing the task you're stuck on, don't stick to the minutiae, try and remember why you're doing the task in the first place.

Focus on high quality output. At the end of every iteration you'll want something usable that you can put in front of stakeholders. It's the job of your team and stakeholders to be able to judge the output of the iteration against the projects goals. You therefore want a finished product in front of you at the end of every iteration.

What do we mean by finished product though? Well, if you are iterating over the design of an interface, that finished product would most likely be something more visual than functional. It would need to be finished though, you wouldn't want the text on a button missing, or some graphics being unrelated placeholders; you want the stakeholders to be able to buy into the vision and therefore everything needs to make sense.

As for web applications, they need to be working and all known bugs fixed. If you get to the end of an iteration and that isn't the case, your team's first job is to admit this and communicate their challenges. They can then pick this up later in their retrospective.

Keep iterations short. If you're focussing on high quality output then keeping to shorter iterations can really help with that focus. By working on a small slice your team can focus on getting that *done* done.

You could choose to tackle the entire checkout in one iteration. However that's a lot of work to complete without receiving feedback. It's also a lot of work to ensure it's done done. It might be easier to take each step in the checkout as an iteration. You might even spend a couple of iterations on each checkout to ensure they're exactly what you need.

Communication is key

Before, during and after an iteration communication will

ideally be maintained between the team and stakeholders. Planning the next chunk of work, giving status updates and presenting a final showcase can all help with communication.

The main purpose for communication is to ensure everyone knows they are working towards the same goals. The team need to coordinate with each other. Stakeholders need to know when the team are blocked so they can help as necessary. Stakeholders also need to give feedback and answer the team's questions.

Stakeholders won't always understand every layer. You may have product owners, or other stakeholders in your business join your stand ups. It is the team's responsibility to remember that the stakeholders may have decreasing levels of understanding as you go down the layers.

Sometimes it might make sense to split your stand up into two or more based on your audience. You don't need to spend any more time than usual, just exclude stakeholders from the really technical implementation details. You can go into the gory details of your deployment failure with the colleagues who understand your pain; spare the Head of Finance.

In order to be respectful to your audience and also provide them understanding, only go into as much detail as they will understand.

Using ceremony to get things done

Many agile practices introduce ceremony. Scrum often includes estimation planning sessions. We already mentioned stand ups. Hopefully everyone is doing retrospectives.

Use showcases to encourage communication, pace and achievement. We like to use showcases during and at the end of iterations. Typically occurring every 2-5 days, the showcase will bring stakeholders and teams together. The team will have a polished showcase that has been well rehearsed and aimed at explaining the value of the work they're producing. The team will end with any questions or blockers they have.

Explaining what goals along with the actual changes made allows the audience to understand the context in which the team have worked and assumptions the team have made. Communication is the main aim and feedback is always desired.

Another benefit of the showcase is encouraging pace. When the team knows a showcase is looming, they will learn to ensure they ready their current changes ahead of time into a polished state. It encourages them to think about the goal and the organisation rather than just cutting code.

Finally, a showcase is a time for the team and stakeholders to celebrate the new value and learnings that the last iteration provided. When everyone champions the process, the process thrives.

Ever changing landscapes

Change is acknowledged and accepted by agile practices. At the end of an iteration we do not necessarily have to continue working with the same set of assumptions in the

the next. When we build out a prototype and realise it's not going to do the job, we can reprioritise our roadmap and adapt for change.

Prioritise by value. Never assume that a roadmap has to be set in stone. It should be fluid and adapt as you work through it. Items in the roadmap will need reordering. Sometimes you'll find a capability isn't even required after achieving a goal sooner than expected. Sometimes a problem you thought you had isn't a problem at all.

If a team sets out to deliver a particular feature over a number of iterations, but realises after the first iteration that what they've produced is releasable, release it! Get users using it. You may find that it quells a need and you might find a different goal or capability to work towards after realising you're getting enough value already.

Acknowledge scope will change. Scope can and should be variable. If your project has a hard deadline, you're going to end up reducing your initial scope. That's almost certain. Acknowledge that the image in your head of the final picture at the beginning of a project will never be the same as what you finally produce.

Have the destination in sight

Not every delivery team will have a project with a deadline. We prefer thinking in a product mindset where delivery is continuous, visions and goals evolving as we go. That said, having a destination in sight is still important.

The initial phases of product development may result in UI/UX artifacts like wireframes or component libraries and these won't necessarily be deployable to end users but should be of high quality. You should aim to get through these phases within a few days or a few weeks at most. You want to be producing software that end users can use and provide you feedback in the form of real data whether that be automatically collect metrics or user surveys.

In a back office environment we aim to be handing over changes to end users every few days, a week at most. Getting things shipped means you can adapt your plan based on feedback. You'll never go too far down a rabbit hole, at most wasting an iteration or two which is a matter of days.

Learn from mistakes with retrospectives, moving fast, your team will make mistakes and that's okay - you'll have great successes too. No matter your flavour of agile, make sure you have regular retrospectives. You might have one at the end of your sprint if you're practicing Scrum. If you're using Kanban you might have one every 2 weeks. Make sure you hold yourselves to account with your actions. Keep a log of all retrospectives and their actions, and always recap on all actions every retrospective until they no longer have value.

Finally, always measure your success against the vision and goals of your delivery. Yes, shipping a new feature means you've put effort in and completed something, but the real success lies in whether that feature provides the desired value.

by Luke Morton

CHAPTER 3
PAIR PROGRAMMING

We've helped a number of organisations successfully adopt pair programming, giving their teams the ability to increase productivity, improve knowledge sharing and enhance the quality of their software.

As a company, we've been using pair programming for around eighteen months, and we've discovered it brings a significant number of benefits, along with one or two challenges we've had to overcome.

In this chapter, we'll be sharing the experiences we've had when introducing pair programming to software teams. We'll then take you through the techniques you'll need to apply what we've learnt to your organisation.

Background

Pair programming was first introduced as part of the Extreme Programming (XP) software development methodology, as an 'extreme' way to practice regular code reviews. Conceived of by Kent Beck in 1999, XP is a collection of software principles which help teams to deliver higher quality software. It places value on communication, simplicity, feedback, courage and respect, all of which, as you'll discover, lead to a positive pair programming experience.

How it works

Pair programming involves two developers sitting at one computer, with one driving, and the other navigating. The driver types out the code, whilst the navigator constantly reviews what is being typed and, at regular intervals, the developers switch roles. Throughout their time together, the pair constantly communicate their thought processes, allowing the other developer to collaborate and help shape the direction of the code.

There are a few guidelines that you should follow when pair programming. These will help you to get the most out of your pair programming experience, and sidestep some of the more common pitfalls we've seen teams experience.

Driving

The driver is solely responsible for typing and controlling the screen. They should externalise their thoughts as they type, and be sure to constantly communicate with their navigator, discussing ideas and clarifying where necessary.

One of the more frustrating aspects of being the driver is that their navigator often has more time to think, meaning they're able to convey their ideas faster than the driver, who is more concerned with typing out code with the right syntax. The driver will often feel clumsy or slow, as the navigator will be able to spot things more quickly than they can. This is OK and to be expected, and the roles switch so regularly that both developers experience the situation from both sides.

Navigating

The navigator is responsible for reviewing everything the driver types, suggesting improvements to the code being written, alternative ways to think about the problem at hand. The navigator should be considerate and careful to minimise unnecessary interruptions when the driver is in flow. Much like a conversation, choose the right moments to point out trivial errors, like spelling mistakes.

Switching

The pair should switch roles to allow each person to get a mix of driving and navigating. There are a couple of methods that are often used to determine switching frequency. One technique is time based, where the developers switch at regular short intervals. Another technique is Ping Pong[2], where developers take turns writing a failing test case, that the other developer then has to make pass.

Taking breaks

Pair programming is intensive, especially over the course of a few hours or a whole day. It's important that pairs don't burn themselves out, so they must make time for regular breaks away from pairing throughout the day. These breaks provide good opportunities to do things that might otherwise distract a developer during pair programming, such as checking emails, instant messaging, or making coffee.

---

2 http://c2.com/cgi/wiki?PairProgrammingPingPongPattern

Pairing, not coaching

Pair programming involves two peers of a similar skill level working together, but it's not uncommon to see some organisations use pair programming as a form of coaching, where a more experienced developer will sit with a less experienced developer and attempt to upskill and explain their rationale around particular design solutions.

There are definite benefits to coaching, but it's important not to confuse it with pair programming, as it can lead to backseat driving, and the less experienced developer becoming demotivated.

Why it works

Modern software delivery has shown us that shorter feedback cycles, frequent communication and regular displays of progress are techniques valuable to any organisation. They help to minimise the risk of a project failing, and they are all inherent in good pair programming.

Programming is hard

We should all know that the most time consuming aspect of software engineering isn't typing, it's the time spent thinking about how to solve the current problem and to design a solution that works well. There are a huge number of choices that need to be considered with every line of code a developer writes, and pair programming helps share that responsibility.

Increased brainpower

Two heads are better than one and, in a pair, each developer will have knowledge in areas the other doesn't, meaning their ability to find good solutions is much better than it would be were they working alone. Additionally, because each idea a developer has needs to meet the approval of their partner, they're forced think a lot more critically about solutions, ultimately leading to better code.

Validation of ideas

Pairing encourages you to explain your thought process as you go, whether you're the driver or the navigator, and in a lot of cases there are several ways to solve a particular problem. By having a partner there to constantly bounce ideas off, you can quickly weed out sub optimal ideas and concentrate on the best solution.

Benefits of pairing

There are many business benefits to pair programming, such as improving the quality of software delivered, building collaboration within a team and helping to share domain knowledge across multiple people.

Productivity and focus

Working so closely with someone else means you've got no other option but to double down on the thing you're working on. The quality of the code becomes a shared responsibility, and means that, when pairing is done properly, you're both driven to produce the best code possible.

The back and forth nature of pair programming also helps to keep you engaged; whether you're switching roles every fifteen minutes, or you've gone the Ping Pong route, navigators are often eager to get back on the keyboard and keep momentum going.

Higher quality

A developer working alone can often be tempted to take shortcuts, either in the interest of time or because they're not quite sure what the best solution is and don't want to feel stuck. It's much more difficult to let that happen when you're working as a pair, because everything you do is being evaluated by another person and you're both responsible for the quality of the code.

Domain understanding

Pairing is a great way to share domain knowledge within an organisation, and makes it much easier for developers to move back and forth across different codebases. By working this way, it means that if a particular developer is absent for any reason, whether it be holiday, sickness, or they've decided to leave, there's at least one other person in the team who has a good understanding of the project and can easily continue working on it.

Improved resiliency

Whatever environment you're working in, the number of things that can interrupt or distract a developer working alone is huge. When you're part of a pair, you become much more resilient to those interruptions because you're both committed to the task at hand. You're less likely to be interrupted by colleagues because they can clearly see that you and your partner are in flow, and you'll more easily resist the temptation to check emails because you're both committed to completing the task at hand.

Team building and cohesion

The stereotypical view of software developers is that they work alone and are poor at communicating with others. Whether or not this stereotype is true, it's not uncommon to find developers who favour working alone and, for teams, this is not ideal.

Pair programming encourages a much more social and collaborative way of working, which helps to build rapport between team members and a culture where your team solves problems collectively.

Learning

The number of technologies and languages within the field of software engineering is vast, so it's inevitable that there'll be areas where one developer is stronger than another.

With pair programming, it becomes much easier for developers to learn from one another as they're being introduced to new concepts as they go.

Continuous code review

Code reviews are a valuable part of any organisation's software development lifecycle. Pair programming takes that concept to an extreme, by having the navigator constantly reviewing what the driver is typing, suggesting improvements or alternate approaches that might help catch edge cases.

Challenges in pairing

Moving from programming alone to becoming a strong pair programmer is not always an easy transition. We've encountered a number of specific challenges which you should watch out for.

Switching mindsets

Programming has historically been a solo activity, so the mindset shift required to work on code together is significant. Developers often struggle to take onboard others ideas and externalise thought processes. This can be particularly challenging if you've worked solo for a long time and are not accustomed to social coding and working closely with others.

People and time

As a business, you shouldn't expect two developers to complete a task in half the time. Often it will take a little longer than if a developer was working alone, so there is a short term cost associated with adopting pair programming. This additional cost is offset by the long term benefits of having higher code quality, less technical debt, and shared domain knowledge.

Exhaustion

Pairing is exhausting. When you've spent the entire day thinking critically about every line of code, justifying and communicating those thoughts and decisions, it's likely that you'll feel drained, but that you've achieved a lot. It's critical that you take regular breaks, that you have some flexibility, and choose appropriate times to pair.

Skill disparity

You'll often find pairing works less well when you've got signifiant skill disparity between a pair. If one engineer is clearly more experienced and is making all the decisions, then this can lead to the less experienced feeling overwhelmed and demotivated, which can lead to disengagement.

Pairing with the wrong people

It's important that developers pair with someone they're well suited to. The most beneficial pairing will be two people who can learn from one another, share similar philosophies and balance each other out.

Backseat driving

When a pair of developers have significant skill disparity, or one member of the pair is louder then the other, then you may encounter backseat driving. This will typically manifest itself in the navigator telling the driver exactly what to type, and the driver following their instructions.

You should encourage the backseat driver to be more considerate, or consider switching the pair members so they are working with people who have similar skill levels.

"Your baby is ugly"

It's important that you are able to communicate honestly with your pair. If one has an idea that the other knows to be bad, they must be capable of saying this and able to present a case for an alternate approach.

Disengagement

Some developers will be resistant to pairing or will spend their time less engaged in the activity. Developers checking their phone constantly, sitting back in their chair or not communicating actively are signs of an individual that is disengaged.

This is detrimental to the team, and it's important to try to understand why it's happening. It may be that the developer really does work better alone, or it's a sign that they're exhausted, there's disparity in skill between them and their partner, or that they simply don't get on with their partner.

Introducing pairing

When introducing pairing to your team, there's a number of things to consider, such as the practicalities, and the typical objections you might face from the business.

Getting started

Start small, take two developers who are keen on the idea of pairing, set them a task to complete and give them the space they need. Get them to champion it, so others can get a sense of how it's working for them.

Have them pair together for a short while, perhaps a couple of weeks, so that they have time to address any teething problems.

Don't assign pairs

Don't force two people to pair together, let pairs form naturally. Keep an eye out for signs of the challenges mentioned above, and provide guidance if it seems like a pair is less effective than it could be.

When not to pair

Not every task requires two developers to tackle it. Having two developers working on the same thing may not be the best use of your team's time; a task may be so straightforward to complete that it relies more on muscle memory than critical thinking, or one developer is tired of pairing and in need of a timeout.

Blockers: "Double the hours"

A popular argument for not adopting pairing is that you're doubling the man hours needed to complete a task, which is simply not true. You're likely to find that the number of man hours does increase, but you'll also find they produce better quality code and spend less time stuck on problems or dealing with technical debt.

Blockers: Management buy-in

Software projects can fail and the most common reason for failure is poor communications or mounting technical debt. Pair programming embeds collaboration into the process, which results in a software product that is of higher quality, and has fewer defects.

When teams engage in pair programming, it means there is less risk when a developer leaves, or is away, as domain knowledge has been spread across the team.

Cynics

It's a hot button topic in software and you'll frequently find people opposed to pairing. You can't force a cynic to engage in pair programming, but you can get the people who are interested in pair programming to evangelise it. Over time, we've found this helps to bring some people around.

Review

As with any agile process, it's valuable to regularly review progress and see if it's working well for your organisation. We've found Agile retrospectives to be a handy tool in helping to understand what has worked well and what may not have worked so well.

Pairing Environments

Workspace and equipment

We see the ideal pairing workstation as having two mirrored screens, plus a shared keyboard and computer. The pairs should be able to comfortably sit side by side with one another in an environment which is ergonomically friendly. At the bare minimum, a pair should have a single computer which they pass back-and-forth.

Remote pairing setup and tools

As remote working has become more popular, tools such as Screenhero have gained traction in the pair programming community, and are a great way to collaborate from different locations.

Unless you're Ping Pong pairing, a Pomodoro app is a must. We use Tomato One, but there are hundreds out there that could be used for pair programming.

Through the increased adoption of open source and a plethora of online tools that help software teams to collaborate, programming has become more social and, with communication being one of the biggest problems in software delivery, we see pair programming as being the natural evolution of this. In fact, many forward-thinking organisations have already adopted the practice, some to the extent that their developers program exclusively in pairs.

by Rory MacDonald & Scott Mason

CHAPTER 4

CODE REVIEWS USING THE PULL REQUEST WORKFLOW

As developers we always appreciate a second pair of eyes and an extra brain. The eyes are really helpful for catching that extra whitespace you might have missed. The additional brain power might help you solve a problem in your code with 5 fewer lines. All of this results in better code and more collaboration.

A way of formalising code reviews within your organisation can be the pull request workflow, which aims to encourage regular code reviews with minimal disruption to your productivity, while gaining tremendous value.

Why code review?

Knowledge share

If you're new to an existing project, what better way to get valuable insight to the workings of it than getting someone familiar to have a look over your changes? It's really difficult to sit and read through the many lines of existing code to fully understand what is available for you to use, but they'll have used existing functions a lot more than you, and will be able to help reduce code duplication.

The code review encourages the start of conversations that lead to improvement of the overall codebase, sharing of best practices and experience from both the reviewee and reviewer.

It's important that reviews are treated as a positive tool. While it's easy to be defensive of your work there's probably a reason a reviewer is suggesting an alternative. In any case, the reviewee should feel comfortable to start a discussion about suggestions provided; it's a good chance to learn.

Developers shouldn't fear having their code picked over, as comments provided should be constructive and it allows to them to gain real insight from their peers. Likewise, a reviewer should always feel comfortable providing constructive criticism if they feel it will lead to improvements.

Visibility

It's one thing for an existing member of the team to join a project, but for new recruits it can be especially daunting. Having frequent code reviews is a great onboarding mechanism to get them involved in the process early on, helping them become familiar with alien codebases.

More often than not, they'll also have new ideas, or other experiences that you can benefit from. Making the code review process as transparent and as open as possible will only encourage this. It also doesn't restrict the conversation to single teams, allowing the wider organisation to have input.

Standards

Code standards aid in readability and maintainability of code. Sometimes standards come in written form, a large set of rules to follow, but other times they're unwritten rules that you'll only really learn the more you develop within an organisation.

This is where that extra set of eyes come in handy.

Ensuring that standards are followed doesn't require much brain power, but they are often easy to miss, especially if you're unfamiliar with them.

Catching these violations early on saves time in the long run and allows everyone to be on the same page, ensuring good readability, and giving the opportunity to open conversations around the standards themselves.

Testing

While a reviewer is normally checking over implementation code, a review offers the opportunity to ensure good practices have been followed while developing code, for example: Test Driven Development (TDD). It's important to make sure tests are present as part of a review if this is a practice your organisation adheres to.

Tests, hopefully, allow the reviewer to follow the design of the implementation while also opening up another area for improvement. Reviews are a great way to ensure that the tests provided are valuable and efficient. An important question to ask here is: do the tests cover all the changes?

Catching bugs

Having another developer look over your work also provides an opportunity to catch any bugs you may not have noticed. While you might have a wonderful, green test suite, a peer might be aware of another edge case within the project that would otherwise have slipped by.

Readability of code

At Made Tech, we feel that if code isn't understandable without comments, this represents a smell. While it's common to see this crop up as a suggestion, is it really required if your functions and variables are clearly and consistently named throughout and have obvious and sensible data returned? Comments can provide value in some cases but they should never be a hard requirement for a code review.

Checklists not required?

While some of the above may look like a checklist, it's not. We're trying more to present some best practices for code reviews, not rules that you have to follow.

We'll dive deeper into this idea as we expand on the value we derive from having adopted a Pull Request Workflow. Some of the things we've covered above can be easily automated to make code reviewing more valuable as a result of this.

Pull request workflow

Pull Requests (PRs) allow for a standard and efficient way of doing code reviews within an organisation. Most popular tools these days, such as Github or Bitbucket, offer features that allow for easy adoption of the pull request workflow.

Adopting the flow

PRs revolve around the idea of using dedicated branches for small feature sets. The branches of work are then submitted to your source control tool, and are opened up for review amongst your team. Only when the majority of people involved are happy with the work will it be merged into your master branch.

Branches

Working in isolated branches reduces the risk of conflicting with the work of other developers. By not working in master, you can remain focused on your goal rather than constantly having to pull in others code.

Single responsibility pull requests

The core idea behind this area is that the less code there is to review the more valuable the review will most likely be. Small features covering only a single area allow for a hyper-focused review and clear understanding of what's trying to be achieved.

A reviewer can easily tell if the tests are present, valuable and covering these small chunks. Working in this style makes it easier for the reviewee themselves to write the tests and feature.

Short lifespans

A great way to avoid merge conflicts with other features and stale code is to impose an arbitrary time limit on a PR. Whether it's a day or just 15 minutes, making sure PRs don't hang around in limbo is an efficient way to maintain momentum on a project.

If more work arrises out of a review don't just stop the conversation, move it out to an issue or multiple issues. Then, assuming everything has been signed off, merge the PR. This allows more time to be spent on the conversation and potentially more opinions to be provided and more thought around the area.

Sign off

While it can be tempting to review your own work if others are busy... don't. This would render the whole process pointless, as it's the extra eyes and brain power you were after in the first place. It would be equivalent to working directly on the master branch.

Try and encourage a culture within the organisation where people are available to comment on PRs as they're submitted, even if they're working on a different project. This encourages having all repositories on Github, and their PRs open to the organisation.

Tooling the flow

We've talked about code standards and tests as part of your review process. These usually follow codified rules that can easily be automated with modern tools and services.

Using your platform fully

Knowing how to leverage your platform for the easiest adoption of this work style is a lot simpler than it may seem at first.

Minor things such as having a clear and brief title and an accompanying description explaining the feature can make it much easier for the reviewer to quickly grasp the purpose of the PR. This can allow them to assess if they have relevant input or want to involve others and also that the feature matches the description provided.

Keeping the conversations around reviews and PRs within the PR itself is the best way to ensure you don't lose any knowledge that surfaces. While it can be easy to take the conversation offline, to email or to Slack, anyone who comes along after will be missing potentially vital context.

Tests and code standards

Github, Bitbucket and other platforms allow integration with 3rd party services or your own Continuous Integration server.

These can be used for automatically running your test suite whenever a pull request is created and updated. This gives constant feedback to the reviewers of a PR, helping them know tests are passing, meaning they don't need to pull down your code and run the tests themselves.

The same can be done for code standards. Linting services are available that can be integrated directly into Github. All of these integrations mean the reviewers can focus on the feature being developed and best practices around the implementation of that code, which is difficult, or impossible to automate.

Notifications

Github has notifications built into their PR functionality. In its simplest form it sends emails for when a PR is created and also when comments are made.

Integration with chat applications, such as Slack, can be added to your Github organisation to give even faster notifications when PRs are ready for review. This can help you have short lived PRs, and when PRs are merged in notifications are sent too.

Optional extras

Github allows protecting branches meaning you can lock down master to avoid anyone pushing to it accidentally. More usefully however, it also allows for PRs to only be merged if the tests and/or linting is in a passing state. While not essential, adopting these extras can help with keeping master safe and secure from accidental commits.

Visibility

Having the ability to look back and see who introduced a feature and the conversation surrounding reviewing it is a valuable way to foster knowledge sharing. If someone is looking to develop a new similar feature or improve upon the original, they can see from the description and conversation why the feature was implemented in this fashion.

We believe using code reviews and pull requests in tandem gives you the most value in terms of time, knowledge shared and potential cost to clients.

The buy-in to adopt this workflow is far less these days because the tools make it far more accessible to the majority. It can be rolled out across a team, a project or the entire organisation.

by Ryan MacGillivray & David Winter

CHAPTER 5
RETROSPECTIVES

At the end of an iteration it's good to take some time to reflect as a team to assess what worked, what didn't work, and what could be improved upon. This can result in future iterations being more efficient and productive, as well as increasing happiness in the team.

At its most basic level, a retrospective is simply having the team sit together and allowing them to voice their opinions on went well and what didn't. This provides increased insight throughout the team. Teams list out each of the points made and then take a vote on which of these are the highest priority. Keeping this to a small list is most prudent as it won't overload the team, and any points that didn't make the list will show up in future retrospectives if they're a persistent problem.

From that list, action points are agreed upon to tackle each item, and the team bears them in mind when going about their day to day business. In future retrospectives, any action points that led to big improvements within a team should be shared back to the organisation as a whole, so that other teams can potentially benefit from learnings.

The Prime Directive

Regardless of what we discover, we understand and truly believe that everyone did the best job they could, given what they knew at the time, their skills and abilities, the resources available, and the situation at hand

- Norm Kerth

It's vital that a retrospective is run in a way where all members feel safe to discuss their viewpoints. Mistakes are something to be celebrated, as they present opportunities to learn, so when describing something that went wrong, be sure not to place the blame at the feet of an individual team member. If someone feels unsafe they're unlikely to be able to fully engage with the retrospective. Violations of The Prime Directive, deliberate or otherwise, should be seen as a team smell and may lead to the team going into the next iteration with a negative mindset.

There are some steps you can take to help maintain safety, such as reminding everyone of The Prime Directive before beginning the retrospective proper, or having facilitators conduct safety/pressure checks.

Safety checks

It's worth running safety checks to gauge how comfortable everyone feels before tackling larger issues. The facilitator should ask each team member to write a number between 0 and 5 on a piece of paper, to mean one of the following:

5 - I'll talk about anything

4 - I'll talk about almost anything, but one or two few things might be hard

3 - I'll talk about some things, but others will be hard to say

2 - I'm not going to say much, I'll let others bring up issues

1 - I'll smile, claim everything is great and agree with authority figures

0 - I'm not comfortable talking/I don't want to do this/I want to leave

Once these have been anonymously collected, the facilitator should tally the count. If there are more low numbers than high they should ask if the team would like the retrospective to continue. Either way there should be a brief discussion as to why the team thinks the numbers are low. If it's decided that the retrospective shouldn't go ahead, then it's worth running this quick exercise to determine why people are feeling unsafe:

- The Facilitator asks everyone to put themselves in the shoes of someone who might not feel safe, then note down what could make them feel that way

- Based on the submitted notes, have the team work together to list reasons that might cause these issues

- Based on the potential causes, ask the team to present and discuss potential solutions

- Run the safety check again

- If the safety level has increased after this point, then you can run the retrospective.

Facilitators

A key role in a retrospective is that of the Facilitator. They contribute feedback along with the rest of the team, but they're responsible for:

- Outlining the retrospective exercise to the team
- Keeping the exercise on track, with a balance of strict time keeping while trying to keep the atmosphere relaxed and informal
- Ensuring the Prime Directive is adhered to
- Helping and prompting thoughts and ideas if the team is struggling
- Reiterating and sharing any agreed upon action points after the retrospective
- Trying to ensure everyone on the team contributes to the discussion

To keep retrospectives fresh and different, try occasionally rotating the Facilitator role so that different members of the team get a chance to define how the session will run.

When deciding upon a retrospective activity, you can choose to go with a tried and tested idea, or something wildly different to help spice things up. We'll discuss some different ideas below, but there are numerous websites out there that provide plenty of ideas to take advantage of.

Scheduling and frequency

We derive the most value from retros when we run them at the end of each iteration (for us this is weekly) directly after a showcase. By running them before the next iteration begins, the team is able to take the learnings and outcomes directly into the following week.

If for whatever reason the team is unable to run one, we've found it best to wait until the next scheduled retrospective, so as to not disrupt the current iteration. Ideally these shouldn't be missed barring illness or holidays. If a team member has contributions to make but can't attend they can choose to provide these to the facilitator ahead of time.

Exercises

To keep energy up in a retrospective and help provide focus to the areas the team aims to cover it's common to use exercises.

These are some of our favourite exercises:

The happiness graph

Ask each team member to draw a graph of how happy they were over the duration of the sprint. The X-axis denotes days, and the Y-axis denotes mood. As moods, we use happy, indifferent, sad and angry, but you may find a different scale works better for you. Have the team chart a line representing their mood over the course of the sprint. When everyone has finished, take the time to discuss any notable peaks and troughs, and make a note of the reasons for each.

As well as being a good way to see how everyone is feeling, with those notes, you can discuss ways you can make sure the things that made people happy continue to happen, and ways to prevent the things that made people unhappy from ever happening.

Hot air balloon

The hot air balloon exercise is popular within our team, with the format being:

- Draw a hot air balloon on a whiteboard or other canvas, with a sun to the right of the balloon, and a storm to the left.

- The Facilitator provides a prompt like "Looking back, what was our hot air, taking us higher, and what were our sand bags, bringing us down?"

- The team then writes these down above and below the balloon as appropriate.

- The team discusses each point as they go to make sure there is a shared understanding.

- The facilitator then offers another prompt "Looking ahead, what stormy weather can we see making the route to our goal difficult, and what steps can we take to move towards sunny days?"

- These suggestions are again mapped to their appropriate area on the drawing, and discussed among the team.

By approaching the retrospective in this way we can reflect on the previous iteration, as well as look ahead to try to avoid any potential pitfalls.

Both of these exercises follow the same outline as the basic idea mentioned earlier. Most exercises work to elicit the following from team members:

- What went badly?

- What went well?

- How can we improve going forward?

Don't let retrospectives become monotonous; mixing these exercises up is an ideal way to keep things fresh and provide different perspectives and prompts to these questions.

Action points

The outcomes of a retrospective can be used to identify action points that can be used to try and enact improvements to the next iteration. In the example of the hot air balloon these would be the items listed featured in the sunny area. Ensuring that these action points are focussed and achievable is essential to their success.

Comradrospectives

Where a standard retrospective is for smaller teams, we've taken to holding a company wide retrospective, known as a Comradrospective. They're an hour long, and we hold them at regular intervals, often two weeks, after each team has had a retrospective. They have the following in common with retrospectives:

- The Prime Directive is read out at the beginning

- A safety check is held before hand

- A facilitator is assigned

- Action points are decided on at the end of the session

These sessions can be focused on a particular topic, or each team can bring discussion points from their retrospectives, to share with the wider company. For example: things that have been holding them back, and their biggest successes. The facilitator of the team retrospective can collate these in advance and propose them to the wider group.

Through sharing and discussing these points as a group the company can identify issues affecting all teams and create further action points to address them. We make a point of revisiting agreed upon action points in future sessions to discuss whether we've been actively focussed on them, and whether they're still a priority for the company.

Customer inclusive retrospectives

Involving stakeholders from the customer side in a retrospective can be a valuable way to both improve communication and provide greater understanding for both sides. This allows for clear feedback from the customer, beyond the scope of a showcase. As well as that, because they can see you're actively taking steps to address any issues raised previously, it strengthens your working relationship.

Retrospectives, in any of their many forms, are an invaluable tool for maintaining healthy, happy software teams. By giving everyone a platform on which to voice their concerns, learn from their mistakes and celebrate their victories, you're ensuring your team will continue to evolve.

by Ryan MacGillivray & David Winter

CHAPTER 6

CONTINUOUS FEEDBACK

We believe it's important to foster an environment of continuous improvement, whereby the performance of every aspect of the organisation is encouraged to be on an upward trajectory.

This is especially true in service and knowledge-based businesses, where, to throw in an early cliche, people are generally your most valuable, or only asset.

What is Continuous Feedback?

The goal of Continuous Feedback is to significantly shorten the personal feedback loop in your teams.

When delivering software, lean and agile tell us to value things like short feedback cycles and regular retrospectives and course corrections. However, for many organisations, the individuals seem to have been sidelined, and the more traditional annual review continues to prevail.

With Continuous Feedback, instead of having a touchpoint every 6 or 12 months, individuals have one every couple of weeks. By focusing on events from the last fortnight, the feedback is more current, and because the next review is only two weeks away, it's an ideal forum for regularly tracking progress on smaller, more incremental goals.

What's wrong with traditional performance reviews?

We perceive a number of downsides to more traditional

performance reviews:

Feedback is not current

If a feedback session happens once every 6 months or, worse, once a year, the time between any event that warrants discussion or course correction can be significant, missing the opportunity to course correct or reinforce that behaviour sooner.

There's also a natural bias to focus more on recent events, rather than potentially more important things that happened 6+ months earlier.

Goals are not tracked regularly

On a similar thread, setting goals to be achieved over the course of a year without more regular opportunities to share progress seldom yields the desired outcome. In the days running up to an annual review you may see a flurry of activity against last year's goals. If there is an opportunity to share progress in the next couple of weeks, it's likely to be a much more current concern.

Feedback season is overly time consuming

For managers with many direct reports, feedback season can be a particularly time consuming period as they try to recall the pertinent events of the previous year. In addition, if the organisation performs '360 feedback' team members need to be badgered, and possibly reminded on how to give good quality feedback.

While it's true that Continuous Feedback likely adds up to more time spent on feedback activity over the course of the year, each feedback window is a less daunting prospect.

Feedback is not owned by the individual

In a traditional review format, where the manager authors or collects the feedback, and it's delivered to the individual, there's little feeling of ownership over the feedback. The individual is almost a passenger in the process. If the feedback is from a third party, the individual may also miss the ability to talk to the feedback giver to better understand its impact.

With these downsides in mind, and with what we can learn from modern software delivery practices, we can consider another approach.

How does Continuous Feedback work?

With the primary goal to shorten feedback loops, Continuous Feedback offers up far more frequent review sessions. For us, once every 2 weeks has proven to be a sweet spot.

These sessions are typically much lighter than a more traditional review, running for somewhere in the region of 15 - 25 minutes per session.

Individual responsible for collecting feedback

With Continuous Feedback, it's the individual who should take responsibility for their own feedback, and for bringing it to the session. This gives the individual more ownership of the process, and also provides them a forum to discuss the feedback with the giver ahead of the session.

We'd generally steer away from anonymising the feedback process, instead trying to encourage a culture where the team is able to provide well thought feedback, and where people are open to receiving such feedback to aid with their personal development.

Short sessions and short-term goals

As mentioned earlier, because Continuous Feedback sessions typically happen much more regularly than more traditional review processes, the sessions themselves are generally much shorter.

Because the next session should be booked in for a couple of weeks time, Continuous Feedback makes short-term goals far more relevant. Individuals can be encouraged to think about the changes they'd like to make in the immediate term based on the feedback they've just received, as well as what incremental steps they can take towards their longer term goals.

The sessions should also provide a forum to add some check-up and holding to account for goals that were set in the previous session. Individuals should be coached to set achievable goals, and there should be an expectation that the majority of these goals will be achieved.

Understand individual dissatisfaction sooner

Review sessions should allow for two-way traffic (though in many organisations they may not!). If an individual is dissatisfied in their role through lack of progress, a lack of enjoyment for the work, having relationship issues with others in their team etc, it's generally far better to hear about this sooner, so it can be rectified before becoming a larger problem.

Sessions can be facilitated by a peer

To encourage more autonomy in teams, it's possible to have peers facilitate each other's review sessions, and further, facilitate sessions for their managers. It can be a useful tool to level out an organisations hierarchy, and to offer another forum for individuals to further develop their softer skills.

In adopting a peer-led structure, organisations may want to consider how any individual dissatisfaction can be fed back to people in the organisation who are able to make changes, if for whatever reason the peer who is facilitating the session is not able to act on it.

So now you've heard about the benefits of Continuous Feedback, how can this be rolled out to your organisation?

How to adopt Continuous Feedback

Continuous Feedback is likely to be a significant change in format for many organisations. The scale of the organisation and how open to change it is will be a large factor in your path to adoption.

That said, one approach almost always provides greatest traction:

Start with a small group

If possible, steer away from launching a 'big bang' change on any sizeable group of people. Our recommendation would be to take a group of 3 or 4 people initially, and introduce the process to them, ideally in the form of a short face-to-face discussion on how you see things working, and why you're keen on giving this a go.

Hand-picking your first cohort can be a good idea - people who are generally receptive and enthused by new ways of working, and people who you think may be good allies to evangelise this process to a wider audience.

After facilitating a Continuous Feedback session for everyone in this group, take the next group of people, and introduce the process in much the same way to them. If you've chosen to adopt peer facilitation, it's a good opportunity to have some of the first group induct the second.

Coach on how to give and receive effective feedback

People in many organisations seldom have the chance to provide feedback, and so may not be well skilled in it.

As the team will be expected to deliver feedback

regularly, and because they'll be delivering that feedback direct to the recipient, it's a good idea to provide some guidance on how to give constructive and actionable feedback.

Equally important is coaching people to receive feedback well. It is likely to be the case that some feedback will talk about areas for improvement for the individual, and so helping people to graciously accept feedback, and ask insightful questions when they don't fully understand the impact can help encourage a more open culture.

Once the feedback has been collated, we need to do something with it.

Encourage ultra-timely feedback

Even with a window of a couple of weeks, it's sometimes hard to keep track of the most pertinent events on which to provide feedback. It can be worth encouraging the giving of feedback as close to the event as possible, so the individual can bring it to their next session.

Givers of feedback may also choose to keep their own journal of feedback they have for other people, so they can quickly recall some recent feedback when asked for it. A word of caution here: if feedback is of a more critical nature, it may be wise to encourage the giver of that feedback to 'sleep on it'. Feedback of such a nature should never be given in the heat of the moment.

Provide a framework for making feedback actionable

During the review session, the individual should bring their collected feedback along.

It's a good idea to provide a framework that encourages the individual to document what impact the event in question had, and what the key points to take-away should be. The role of the facilitator should be to bounce ideas off, and to ask questions to help the individual to think more deeply about the feedback.

Once the feedback has been discussed, it's a good idea to look at some goals. Discussing progress towards the previous goals, closing out wherever possible, and identifying any new goals, either based on course corrections from the feedback, or as smaller increments towards the individuals longer-term goals. The facilitator should be doing what they can to hold the individual to account in achieving these short term goals.

Keep momentum up

As with any organisational initiative, keeping momentum remains a challenge. In the hustle of day-to-day work, it can be easy to allow commitments such as this to drop.

You can consider rewarding buy-in from those who perform best at keeping their commitment high, offering public recognition, a company lunch or some other soft benefit. These people can be good allies in encouraging similar from their peers.

Encouraging individuals, when asking for feedback,

to highlight particular areas they're focusing on can help people provide more relevant and actionable feedback.

In much the same way as retrospective exercises provide different formats with generally similar outcomes, you can occasionally switch up the format of the review session to keep things fresh.

Overcome resistance

When rolling out any change to an organisation, you're likely to meet some pockets of resistance. These are some of the common arguments we've seen:

HR won't let me do this

In larger organisations, HR may be a large skills silo with autonomy over how such things work. If you're unable or unwilling to fight this battle, you can run Continuous Feedback in parallel in your own team. You might have to continue to adhere to the more traditional approach provided by your HR team, but at least you'll have generated and documented plenty of feedback throughout the year to feed in to that process.

Shouldn't managers manage?

Some organisations are precious over the hierarchy of managers managing people. It's possible to pick and choose how you want your implementation of Continuous Feedback to work - it's entirely possible for managers to facilitate all of the sessions, for example.

As a principle, we'd be encouraging devolution of everything reasonably possible to the team, but that's a discussion for another chapter.

How can we let people go?

Without the paper-trail of objective setting and measurement that more traditional approach offers, Continuous Feedback could be said to be a poor means by which to manage business exits. We believe such events aren't the norm, and so should be managed by other means.

Our observations

We've been practising Continuous Delivery for some time. There are a number of hurdles or downsides that we've observed.

More employees buy into it than others

As with many initiatives, it's likely that some people will be more enthused than others. Some people can become anxious when expecting to receive overly-negative feedback (which seldom turns out to be the case), while others value the opportunity to have regular personal course correction discussions.

Poor forum for larger issues

If there are larger issues afoot with an individual, Continuous Feedback is not a good forum for dealing with them. This remains a good forum in which to involve a HR specialist.

Without monitoring it's easy for people to duck under the radar

Particularly where the program is largely delivered by peers, without some sort of tooling in place to increase visibility on the review schedule, some people may go for longer periods without a review.

Struggle to keep accountability around short term goals

A potential downside to delivering the sessions with peers, is that some accountability on goals can be lost. Some people are less comfortable in holding individuals to account on their achievement of their goals.

We believe Continuous Feedback to be a logical next step for teams who have been working hard to shorten feedback loops around their software delivery, and who have been practising team retrospectives as a part of their development cycle.

If nothing else, it forces teams to have more conversation about individuals growth and development objectives, and provides a regular forum for people to vent their frustrations with a co-worker. The agile manifesto reminds us to value individuals and interactions, after all.

by Chris Blackburn

CHAPTER 7
RECOGNITION & REWARD

Morale is closely related to job satisfaction. When morale is high, your team is happier, more productive, and more likely to believe in your organisation's vision. On the flip side, not enough (or any) praise for a job well done, dealing with difficult clients, or heavy workloads can significantly lessen morale, and sometimes lead to higher employee turnover.

In this chapter we'll discuss the importance of morale and how you can identify when levels are moving in an unfavourable direction, as well as how to give teams a boost by taking the time to recognise, and possibly even reward, their efforts.

Recognising low morale

Identifying the root cause of low morale can be complex, with a number of contributing factors. It is a situation that no organisation wants to be in as it has significant costs down the line: quality of the product suffers, clients become unhappy and there is no energy within the team.

Reasons morale drops

There are various reasons for morale dropping within a company, and the following are some of the more common causes.

Poor leadership

Teams should be given the opportunity to self direct and

self organise, so that they're better able to complete tasks, engage with customers and work together. That said, teams still need direction from a leader, and without that, teams can begin to feel unimportant, as though what they're doing has little worth.

Poor communication

Everyone needs to be kept in the loop with what's going on in the current project. Goals, praise, performance or personal gripes will always arise and need to be communicated within the team. Team members also need to be upfront with each other.

The last thing you want is a disengaged workforce where individuals feel left out and undesirable social hierarchies start to form. There's a lot you can do to help promote communication amongst teams, and we've discussed it at length here.

Unresolved conflict situations

The act of creating software is a very subjective topic and, given the speed at which the software industry moves and new technologies are introduced, conflict situations are sure to arise when opinions clash. Dealing with these conflicts and others is critical to maintaining morale, as lingering resentment over unresolved conflicts leads to a break down of trust between team mates, and can also lead to a fear of any kind of workplace conflict.

Lack of empowerment or autonomy

If you do not allow your team to take ownership of a feature, they will take less pride in it. Here at Made Tech we believe that programmers should be responsible for delivering features end to end. This means dealing with all aspects of it from communication with clients, to infrastructure and programming. If you only deliver a very small slice of this, you will not appreciate the positive impact that you are having on the problem, which may lead to dissatisfaction.

Heavy workloads

Bad estimates and poor planning can result in significant workloads on individuals. No one wants to work overtime, especially if they are not being compensated for it. Failing to understand the underlying requirements of a piece of work can have drastic consequences on the amount of work that is required to be completed. An overburdened workforce may also be a sign of significant understaffing, and as such is a problem that needs to be rectified sooner than later.

Poor working conditions

A team cannot do their best work in an environment not equipped to handle their needs. Without a space that allows them to collaborate, communicate, focus and relax, your team will become increasingly dissatisfied and more prone to distraction.

Knowing how and why a team's morale drops is the

first step in making their happiness a priority, but beyond simply trying to prevent such a negative outcome, there are plenty of positive moves you can make to raise morale, and it starts with recognising the effort your team is putting in.

Recognition

A downside of only having individual recognition is that it can introduce competition. To receive recognition, you must excel compared to your colleagues. Unfortunately, this can lead to unhealthy environments and slow degradation of teamwork.

By contrast, cultures with only full team recognition lead to a marked increase in amounts of cooperation and collaboration, as this is the only way to achieve success. The downside of team-only recognition is that it can go awry when individuals begin to feel that underperformers are receiving just as much reward for their actions.

Another solution seen in other cultures is never to recognise anyone for fear of causing these problems. It is important to consider that this will begin to cause individuals to feel unvalued.

Although we value individual recognition, we favour team recognition. We also believe that people should be recognised primarily through ad-hoc channels, by their peers, not by whoever sits above them in the hierarchy. We use Continuous Feedback as a platform for this recognition. It's important to recognise the highly positive impact that recognising teams and individuals has on morale and, potentially more importantly, the disturbing implications of poorly handling mistakes as well.

Handle mistakes in a positive way

In a high safety, high trust environment, with practices such as Continuous Feedback and retrospectives, the detection of a mistake should not be seen as an opportunity for a chastising or otherwise attacking the individual(s) responsible for that mistake.

Morale can be boosted during periods of adversity too, through robust, mature methods for picking up the pieces after a mistake has been made. Using mistakes as opportunities to engage in positive learning and improvement experiences, rather than downtrodden experiences, makes people feel both happier and supported in their role.

Not to mention that as a leader, you can be more effective in your role when individuals feel they can share their mistakes openly and freely with everyone else. The reason is simple: the entire team can learn how to avoid making that mistake in future. By contrast, in environments where individuals are incentivised to cover their mistakes, from fear of retribution, then the wider team misses out on the learnings gained.

Communicate openly

Agile values communication with customers highly. A team should be driven to do the things that build customer happiness, with the hope that they are delighted by the team's efforts. Since this is the case, teams that work in close collaboration with customers have the benefit of receiving that praise directly. This praise, when received as part of a tight feedback loop with the customer, can be used as an early warning sign that something is not quite right when the amount of praise decreases.

Peer recognition

Recognition has a half-life. One consideration of solely using annual reviews as an opportunity for recognition and praise is that these cultures risk leading to large dips in morale. As an alternative, spreading recognition throughout the year, with a platform for peer-to-peer recognition in place ensures there is never the opportunity for such dips.

At Made Tech, we have "Made Merits", a form of Karma system that is used to reward good deeds on a peer-to-peer basis. A consideration of using such a platform is that it can lead to a dip in intrinsic motivation, this can be initially manifested by "will you give me a Merit if I do that" but also demotivation when a Merit isn't received. While we believe that "Made Merits" are a harmless part of our culture, it is possible to draw parallels between Merits and other extrinsic motivators.

Recognise dependence on recognition, an extrinsic motivator, and ensuring they are also finding their work intrinsically rewarding is something that only the individual team member can do by themselves.

Reward

Having recognised and acknowledged the great work your team has done, it's time to talk about the ways in which teams and individuals can be rewarded. As we see it, rewards can be either extrinsic, something that either is or costs money, or intrinsic, something that lends itself to helping the people being rewarded feeling fulfilled and happy.

Intrinsic

Arguably the more powerful type of reward is the intrinsic reward. It's also the trickier to give, since these rewards are something teams need to feel, rather than be given, and you can't force people to feel a certain way.

Purpose

By making a point of monitoring and keeping morale up, along with creating communicative environments where their hard work can be recognised, allowing your team to structure the way they work, giving them ownership of delivery and many of the other practices we've discussed, the members of your team will feel a sense of purpose, a sense that they, and the work they're doing, matters.

With a sense of purpose, a team knows why what they're doing is important, they're driven to do it, and to do it well. Understanding how their work feeds into the wider company objectives plays a big part of instilling a sense of purpose, and we found it particularly useful to define a company mission in order to clarify why the company exists and what we're trying to achieve.

Each of our teams knows our company mission is to improve software delivery in every organisation, meaning every member of said teams believes in our mission, and anybody joining us wants to help us achieve it.

Freedom to learn

We're proud of the work we do with our customers, but every software engineer loves having the freedom to go off and get stuck into a technology that interests them, and the two things don't always align. Rather than snuffing that thirst for knowledge out, giving your team the space to pursue and share their interests is an excellent way to keep morale up, and may even yield benefits for the wider organisation down the line.

At Made Tech, the entire team often engages in a number of non customer focussed activities, such as code dojos and hack days, where we set aside an hour a week or an entire day every month or so for everyone to do something fun and interesting that doesn't necessarily have to have commercial benefits.

This creates an environment where every member of the team knows they have the freedom to suggest other ways in which to promote learning, and that their team will respond positively to their suggestions. A recent example is the "Code Roast", a variation on the traditional practice of code reviews, whereby a team member will pull out a piece of code they're particularly not proud of, present it to the rest of the team, who spend an hour pointing out its flaws and then working together to improve it.

Fresh challenges

For organisations like ours, who work on a variety of different projects for different customers, having a team stay on one project for months on end can become tiresome, leading to a loss of productivity and enthusiasm.

While it's beneficial to have somebody on the project throughout the engagement, if only to help build and maintain a relationship with the customer, we've found it important to let our teams know that, if they have a burning desire to do so, they have the opportunity to change things up at semi-regular intervals throughout the year.

A team member can choose to either stick, and stay on the project they're on, or twist, so that they can pursue a fresh challenge. Knowing that you're not shackled to a particular project for what could be years is liberating, and keeps things feeling fresh.

Extrinsic

On the other side of the coin are extrinsic rewards. These are things the company can give to teams to both celebrate their work, and also to maintain a healthy level of morale. While we're not advocating showering them with gifts, we do see benefits to treating your team beyond just material gains.

The following are two examples of situations we've felt it was important to hand out extrinsic reward; there are many other appropriate ways to reward your organisation, you just need to find what works best for you, your team and your organisation.

Company Retreat

Recently, having had a particularly successful year which saw the company grow in many positive ways, thanks to the combined efforts of the entire Made Tech team, it was decided that, for the first time since the company was founded, everybody would be taken on a company retreat.

This took the shape of a 5 day break in Spain, where we'd spend a few hours each day building a product we'd use internally, and then hanging out in the evenings. This could be seen as both an extrinsic and intrinsic reward; everything was paid for by the company, but we used the building of the project as another opportunity to learn, and the entire experience was a great team building activity.

Celebrating success

Whether it's successfully launching a project, completing an engagement with a customer, or your team has reached a landmark point during the engagement, it's important to recognise these moments and celebrate them. These moments only come about because the entire team pulled together to produce the best work they possibly could, and letting those efforts go unnoticed is a sure fire way to leave your team feeling deflated. Whether it's something as simple as a trip to the pub for a few team drinks, or something more extravagant, celebrate the achievements your team is responsible for.

It goes without saying that your team is vitally important.

Without them, nothing gets done, so making sure your team feels happy, fulfilled and committed to their goals should be near the top of your organisation's list of priorities. By taking the time to check in with your team and gauge how they're doing, listening to what they have to say and recognising the efforts they're putting in, you're creating a positive environment for everyone within the organisation.

by Craig Bass, Scott Mason & Emile Swarts

Part 2: Quality

Having given your teams the tools they need to improve communication both amongst themselves and within the wider organisation, you need to ensure that those teams are capable of delivering quality software.

A team is made up of individuals, and each individual will inevitably have their own way of working, which can lead to competing or conflicting opinions on the best way to proceed with the tasks at hand. Discussion is important, and helps the learning process, but by establishing a framework for quality, you can steer that discussion to a place that promotes both learning and better software.

In this next section, we'll discuss practices you can put into place that will ensure quality is not only maintained but continuously improved upon, through techniques like giving teams the responsibility of delivering the software they've built, and learning how to react positively to mistakes and failures.

CHAPTER 8

GIVE TEAMS OWNERSHIP
OF DELIVERY

It's a poorly kept secret that increasing levels of responsibility, particularly with knowledge workers, often correlates to an increase in performance.

We strive to have the team dedicated to a software product responsible and accountable for the end-to-end delivery: from initial requirements capture, right through to launching and supporting the application.

In devolving responsibility to teams, there are a number of areas worth consideration, the first of which is what skills you'll need on the team to best achieve this.

Shaping the team

When pulling together a new team, it's important to consider the blend of skills that you need. We tend to shy away from specialist roles, such as database administrators or dedicated testers, though we do see value in ensuring a healthy mix of experience levels on a team.

We package desirable behaviours in to documented traits, describing a series of attributes people can work towards. One of these traits is delivery, which encompasses process improvements, understanding commercial objectives, and ensuring customer needs are met. Other organisations may choose to recognise related attributes in other ways, such as through team lead or similar titles. Whatever your flavour, it's sensible to consider having an experienced pair of hands in the team with the nous to nudge things in the right direction.

On the flipside, it's wise to be wary of conflict in teams where everyone is chasing the same personal objective. If you have multiple people on the team who are used to playing a delivery lead role, the team may not easily settle. Having a mix of people skilled in a number of different areas who can coach and upskill other members in their various strengths is a positive place to be.

Once you're confident you have the right mix of people together, the next step is to consider how to better empower them.

Empowering the team

Successful team empowerment typically comes from blending expectations, responsibility, and accountability. Without these forces working in balance, you're likely headed for frustration.

It's firstly important to instil a sense of responsibility that everything from understanding what the customer needs, right through to launching the thing in production is down to the team.

Depending on the culture in your team and wider organisation, you may need to do some work to set expectations on what you expect the team to be achieving. This should shy away from task-level goals, but be a higher level goal - perhaps something along the lines of: increasing customer happiness through delivering valuable, working software regularly.

Once you've done this, your next step is to not interfere. For many managers, this part is particularly tricky.

Your only responsibility from here on in should be to hold the team to account for meeting their commitments and for delivering to the higher-level expectations that you've agreed. We cover accountability in a little more detail later.

An empowered team should be focusing its efforts on problems, not on implementing perceived solutions provided by an external architect or other higher being.

Task teams with problems, not solutions

Ensure that the team are being engaged at the correct level. If you're looking to encourage strategic, rather than just tactical skills, don't ask the team to deliver a pre-defined solution to the problem.

Instead, ensure the team are empowered with, and are actively seeking out, an understanding of the commercial goals behind each and every feature.

Have the team take responsibility for identifying and then delivering solutions to these commercial problems, rather than executing against a pre-baked task list. This ownership of the fuller problem should help accelerate a feeling of empowerment.

When relinquishing any kind of control, or when trying to increase the empowerment of others, it's highly likely that many things will not be done as you would have done so yourself, and it's important to quickly come to terms with this.

Be prepared to accept mistakes

If you were managing a task-list for a team and having them

execute it, it's likely you're going to be getting your own way a lot of the time. When a team moves to working toward higher order goals, this is likely to not be the case.

It's important to be prepared to accept that mistakes will be made. Wherever possible, you'll need to allow the team the freedom to do this, even where there's a cost involved, and where you believe you can clearly foresee the problem.

If you're overly keen to jump back in and provide input, you'll too easily undo the work involved in imparting a true sense of responsibility and empowerment, and before you know it, members of the team will be deferring decision making outside of the team.

You should try to see your role as preventing the team from jumping off a cliff, but not much more. Opening yourself to the right conversations can help a seasoned leader more easily accept this transfer of decision making.

This topic is discussed more fully in Chapter 10.

Ensure you're being asked the right questions

Particularly with newly empowered teams, you should make yourself open to discussing strategies with the team. However, you should be careful to avoid allowing the team to too easily devolve lower-level decision making your way.

A quick and easy technique is when asked a question, first ask the other person what they think the best course of action is. Even if you'd consider doing things differently, unless you believe what's being proposed is significantly detrimental, let the team run with it without providing input.

You should move to a mindset of providing advice from outside of the team. One easy tactic to accelerate this shift is to ensure the day-to-day point of contact is inside the team.

Point of contact

In most engineering teams, it's natural for there to be a primary point of contact for the Product Owner, Customer, or similar role. It's of paramount importance that this primary day-to-day contact be someone in the team, rather than having communication fed through intermediaries, particularly those more senior within the organisation, and those not full-time committed to the engagement.

Having communication come from a conduit outside the team disempowers the team from building direct relationships with those commissioning the software, and it hinders open conversations that help engineers better understand the true commercial objectives and pressures.

The point of contact is unquestionably an important role within the team, particularly if you provide consultancy-like services to other organisations. You should be conscious to invest in upskilling, nurturing, and providing regular support to those new to this role.

Upskilling the team

There are a number of areas in which you could consider

upskilling the team, particularly if increased responsibility and empowerment is new for them.

Delivery mindset

If someone has spent much of their time being assigned tasks, and then executing them, it's likely some work is needed to coach more of a delivery mindset.

This involves thinking at a higher level about how to best move from a stated problem, to working, released software. Likely this will entail higher level of communication with customers, helping shape priorities, identifying and articulating solutions, and ensuring there's an appropriate framework in place to facilitate fast delivery and fast feedback.

Customer service

Many organisations make the mistake of hiding their engineers away from the customer, instead relying on a middleman to collate requirements, showcase the software, and generally keep the customer happy.

You should encourage a solutions-focused culture, where engineers see their role as facilitating the customer, be it an internal or external stakeholder, in achieving their commercial goals. Ensuring regular and open communication, and regular showcasing of the software can go a long way.

In many organisations, if software engineers have historically been engaged later in the process, after pre-conceived solutions have been devised, there can be a pervasive 'no culture', where engineers will not be used to engaging in the process of helping to solve higher order problems. In these cases, additional effort will be required to shift the culture to one of more open, helpful dialogue.

Understanding the problem

If your team have historically been focused more on solving task-based problems, coaching is likely to be necessary to help in how to better gain an understanding of the higher level problem to be solved. Consider encouraging communication with the end user, support in navigating organisations to reach the true stakeholders, and relentless questioning of why requirements are important.

Commercial understanding

In some organisations, you may observe engineers shielded or otherwise isolated from the commercial drivers behind software deliveries. In the worst cases, which are thankfully a little less common nowadays, engineers can be tasked with building libraries with specific interfaces, with no understanding of what's going to be interacting with this interface, even at the software level, let alone the higher-level commercial goal it's designed to solve.

Instead, we believe people perform best when they understand the domain in which they're working, and when they understand the commercial goals that the software is supposed to solve. Empowered with this understanding, coupled with their software engineering know-how, engineers can often propose easier and cheaper solutions to achieve the same aim.

To ascend a team to true autonomy, healthy mechanisms need to be in place to keep accountability levels high. Without them, the temptation for managers to interfere often become too great.

Keeping teams accountable

An important, sometimes overlooked, trait when increasing ownership within teams is putting in place appropriate mechanisms to hold the team to account for unacceptable deliveries.

As a consequence of empowering the team with higher level responsibilities, you'll often see teams naturally holding themselves to higher account. This is the ideal culture to be building.

That said, it's likely that, given enough iterations, even amongst teams who have plenty of experience with higher levels of empowerment, there will be occasions where less desirable performance will be observed and should be surfaced.

To avoid disempowering the team, it is suggested to give higher level feedback, and to allow the time to digest and work out solutions without taking involvement. Describe the situation that you observed as undesirable, and explain the reasons you feel this way.

You should use this mechanism sparingly, as its effectiveness is likely to be reduced the more you lean on it. If you find it necessary to follow this recourse every week or so, it's likely you've got larger root problems that need to be addressed, or that you're not truly comfortable in allowing the team to be fully empowered.

This feedback should be given at an arms length, avoiding the temptation to roll your sleeves up and become a part-time team lead.

Supporting teams from the outside

While a large part of encouraging ownership is allowing teams to operate more autonomously, it's important to also offer an appropriate level of support.

You should keep front of mind that you need to provide this support from outside of the team to avoid undermining the team's autonomy.

Ideally, you want to encourage a culture where a team will proactively ask for help or input when they feel they need it. Offering up too much assistance can have an undermining influence, even when well intended.

Aim to always ask the other person, or the team, how they think to best handle the situation before offering up your own solution, further nurturing independent thinking.

The nature of the team and the individual will dictate the best way to provide support. For some people, carving out a small dedicated amount of time each week may provide a good forum for supporting, for others, you may find you naturally have more informal conversations throughout the day.

Next steps

Depending on where your teams currently are on the spectrum of empowerment dictates how much effort will be needed to give teams full ownership of their deliveries. As with rolling out any organisational change, we'd recommend to introduce change progressively and subtly, beginning by exhibiting and coaching the behaviours yourself.

If you're currently integral to the delivery of software projects, particularly in cases where you're not truly a part of the full-time team, you should consciously look for opportunities where you can transfer these responsibilities to the team.

With teams taking on more autonomy, not only are you likely to reap the benefits of people feeling more responsible, more valued, and more productive, you're also building a foundation that allows you to scale engineering efforts across many autonomous teams.

by Chris Blackburn

CHAPTER 9

KEEPING QUALITY HIGH

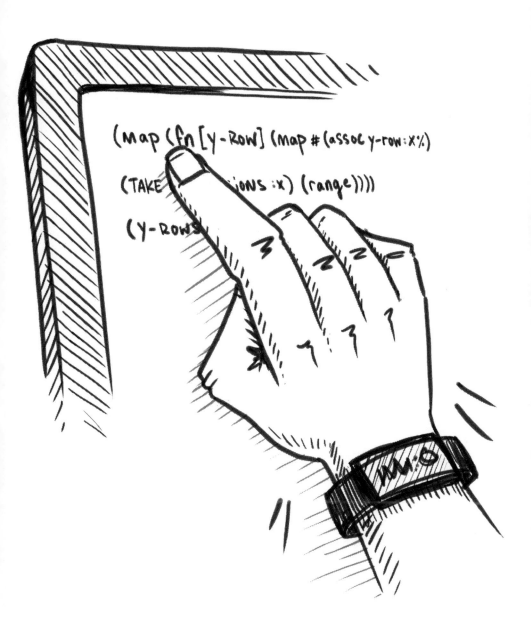

Code quality is a term that is often thrown around in the software engineering industry. Like the art of coding itself, it is very subjective and its true meaning will differ depending on an individual, or a particular team's beliefs. At its heart, most engineers and teams would agree that good quality code is easy to read, well tested, and maintainable in the long term. But how do we achieve this?

It starts with a feature

Often a client will present what they see as the solution to a problem, guised as a feature request. However when a team takes their first slice into this feature, they should not do so blindly.

If there are big questions about functionality, or end-user requirements, these unknowns should be uncovered. This will enable the team to build a better solution, with the least amount of code possible. Ultimately, this alone will increase code quality; less code means a smaller codebase which leads to a more manageable system in the long term.

From the outset understanding the shape of a feature keeps the team laser focused, meaning everyone has a clear definition of success for a task. Although an initial slice may have been defined, teams should not be in fear of changing it's requirements if during the course of an iteration they find a cleaner approach.

Next we commit

At Made Tech, we use pull requests on all of our projects,

meaning we work on new code in a separate branch and request review before merging it and releasing it. We deliberately keep changesets small, releasing small increments of the feature early and often. We work this into our version control and code review workflow in a practice we call "Single Responsibility Pull Requests".

This practice avoids "Big Bang" deployments, where many changes have been made since the last production deploy, introducing many points of potential failure, rather than just one. Releasing continuously hopefully means our pathway to production is always clear. This is a fundamental principle behind continuous delivery.

Furthermore, smaller changesets are easier to digest, so when we request code review, reviewers are able to do a better job. They have more room to comment on particular areas, asking questions or suggesting improvements, if they only have to look over 10 lines, rather than 100. We can be sure that they properly understand the code we've implemented if they only have to look at a small chunk. Many changes over many files with many concerns can get confusing. The reviewer doesn't necessarily know what all the parts do and making sense of the whole thing can be intimidating. Massive cognitive overload leads to poor reviews. Poor reviews leads to bad code getting into the codebase, reducing quality.

Make sure you break large features down into smaller slices. Write these in a way that they can be deployed individually rather than as a massive chunk whenever possible, and don't block the route to production. Request code reviews continuously during development to ensure reviewers can understand the feature throughout, rather than trying to make sense of it at the end, and always make sure they're satisfied before merging it.

Raising the bar

Keeping code quality high through manual code review is great and a really worthwhile practice, but it is often not so good for static code analysis. Static code analysis is another vital way we at Made Tech keep our code quality high, and machines are much better at doing this than humans.

Static analysis can be broken down into a number of areas like complexity, style and security, and there are many tools that deliver this functionality. For raising the standard of your codebase the primary focus should be ABC complexity.

ABC complexity is counting the number if assignments, branches and conditions within a method or function. A high ABC metric is a good indicator that the code is doing too much and should be broken down in to smaller, easier to understand chunks. It's important to stress that keeping ABC complexity low doesn't always mean you have an easy to understand codebase. The metric also doesn't reward terse code, instead it prefers simple code.

Arguably our most favoured practice at Made Tech is TDD, test driven development, which is writing tests before writing code. This has broad benefits across code, but especially code quality. Like having a defined objective for a task, TDD keeps you focussed on accomplishing it, and ensures you're not writing perfunctory code. Every line you write is necessary to bring the feature closer to completion.

This not only ensures you're writing the right code, it

ensures the code you write is maintainable over time, preventing regressions down the line. Engineers in future don't need to be afraid when making changes the codebase if they're confident that it's well tested. They can trust that if they break anything, the test suite will fail, and they'll be able to fix it before it gets into a production environment. To accomplish this we include an accompanying test in every PR.

Keeping it high

We are committed to our projects and maintain them diligently over their lifetime, so it is in our best interests to invest time in quality. Although ensuring projects start off properly is paramount, making sure they stay in good shape and quality remains high is even more important, so we employ a number of practices and tools to enforce standards over time.

One way we do this is through style linting. Style linting is another form of static analysis that requires your code to be written in a certain way, as predefined by either a language, or an opinionated community standard. For example at Made Tech we use StyleLint, ESLint, and Rubocop among others.

This means over the lifetime of a project the code can only be written in a certain way, so it will stay consistent. Linters will often suggest better ways of doing things, progressively upskilling the team in a language. This is extremely helpful when onboarding team members who are less familiar with a language. It also makes people feel they are delivering high quality code whilst still learning.

However, style linting should not be seen as a silver bullet, as it doesn't always lead to high performant code, sometimes aesthetics have to be sacrificed for efficiency. Additionally, style configuration is highly subjective. At the end of the day it comes down to an individual's beliefs. People in the same team may have different ideas about how code should look, and you may even rely on third party defaults for code style rather than defining your own. What's important is that code remains consistent.

Forcing developers to run all these code quality tools themselves can be a drag, but we want to ensure they're always run before code is merged in, so we automate their inclusion in our workflow. We use PaaS services like CircleCI to automatically run our test suites, static analysis tools and security testing against commits and pull requests in Github. This means code reviewers don't need to worry about these elements, as they have to succeed in order for the PR to be eligible for merging.

Additionally, running these quality assurances means an engineers approach to code continuously improves. Spotting failures due to bad code soon becomes second nature. This then has the benefit that, as they maintain the project, when they encounter new areas of the project they are able to bring that code up to scratch, or at least leave it cleaner than they found it. Essentially, code should not be seen as sacred and while an engineer can be protective of code they have written they should also not be afraid of deleting or even replacing code when the time comes.

As with code bases, so should teams be ever changing, since this also leads to greater code quality. A fresh set of eyes will spot problems an incumbent engineer will just live with, if they have noticed them at all.

First and foremost, a well tested, easy to read codebase is easy to maintain. Employ automated quality tools to ensure the code your team writes today and the code they write next year is excellent. Deliver features one chunk at a time to ensure code reviews are diligent and comprehensive, without demanding high cognitive load. Write automated tests and run them on every change to defend against regressions and let your tests document functionality, rather than trying to maintain documentation that can go stale.

Engineers often consider code they wrote last month to be the worst in the world. That will probably never change, because as engineers we're always learning and improving. However, if quality is always kept high, whilst beliefs may change, we can always be proud of the code we have written.

by Seb Ashton

CHAPTER 10
LEARNING FROM MISTAKES

As software engineers, we're faced with new problems and challenges every day. No matter how well we know a programming language, how many projects we've worked on throughout our careers or how much time we've spent creating repeatable solutions to common problems, there will always be something new that requires critical thought.

Inevitably, then, we will make mistakes. Deadlines will not always be met, solutions may not always be correct, and critical tasks may be overlooked. We may even accidentally break the software. These are not Bad Things.

When we're walking an unfamiliar path, we're bound to make the occasional wrong turn. What's important is that we know that those mistakes have a lot to teach us, and that we're in an environment where it's safe to make those mistakes.

Creating a safe environment to fail

Avoiding Blame

From an early age, we're taught that when we do something wrong, there are negative consequences. We learn to associate those consequences with the action that caused them, and we actively avoid it in future. We're also encouraged to assign blame when we see others doing something wrong, if only to again avoid negative consequences directed at us.

This continues into adulthood and our careers, with the assumption being that your employees work as hard as they do to, in part, avoid making mistakes and being made an example of. The belief is that without negative consequences to failure, your employees will be less engaged and less motivated.

This attitude is counterproductive to a healthy working environment. Giving your team a space in which mistakes and failures can be accepted and learned from doesn't mean encouraging lower standards, but ensuring your team and your organisation as a whole can continue to evolve and grow.

It's also important to recognise that mistakes and failures are not necessarily the result of wilfully deviant behaviour. Tolerating mistakes, and recognising that they are opportunities for everyone to learn rather than for one person to be blamed, is a skill.

Retrospectives

Your team needs to know that mistakes can be tolerated, and the best way to convey this is to have open discussions about problems that have arisen, without playing the blame game. Take the time to talk about why a mistake happened. Once you've discovered the mistake, you need to find out what it can teach you and how it can help you in the future.

As mentioned in Chapter 5, the Prime Directive of retrospectives illustrates perfectly the attitude that should be taken when trying to create an environment that looks at mistakes and failures in a positive light.

Retrospectives happen at the end of a sprint, usually every week or two, and give everyone a platform on which to highlight things that went well, and things that didn't go so well. Providing you've built an environment in which it's safe to be honest about shortcomings and mistakes, retrospectives are a great way to uncover process failures and to voice concerns about the work that may lead to avoidable mistakes.

An example we've encountered is realising that our mistake was not getting enough detail on requirements during the planning stage. This led to us moving down a path of work that we ultimately discovered was incorrect when we presented it to the customer.

Within the subsequent retrospective, we were able to safely discuss this as a team, and to admit that there were things we could have done but didn't. We spent time figuring out why this had happened, and then deciding on actionable steps we could take to prevent it happening again in future. We came away from the retrospective having realised we needed to spend more time early on discussing requirements with the customer, and then making sure that information was disseminated across the entire team.

Embracing mistakes

We're in the discovery business, and the faster we fail, the faster we'll succeed.

- Amy Edmondson[3]

The best way to deal with mistakes and failures is to treat them as opportunities to learn, both individually and as a team, after all, while it's our job to design solutions that

---

3 https://hbr.org/2011/04/strategies-for-learning-from-failure

meet requirements, we're not infallible. When we're embarking on a new challenge, making mistakes is a crucial part of the discovery and experimentation process.

Our solutions may fail in unforeseen ways, or we may need to revisit the task and find that we've made more work for ourselves by creating something inefficient. Either way, you have the opportunity to reflect on what went wrong, why, and how you can simplify the process to either reduce or eliminate mistakes.

Big mistakes are easy to spot and discuss. In software, you know something's gone wrong if, for example, a build fails, critical data is lost or a website goes offline. Steps are immediately taken to fix those mistakes and resume normal service. The trick is being able to identify and learn from smaller mistakes, as they're much more easily hidden, both passively and actively. The earlier these are discovered, the better.

This mindset of actively discussing and learning from mistakes, rather than blaming anybody for them, doesn't mean you're encouraging your team to slack off and take shortcuts to the detriment of the project. Even in situations where a mistake can be attributed to an individual's lack of care or inattentiveness, there's the chance to dig deeper and discover what led to that behaviour, and what you can do to improve the situation for the individual and your team.

Using mistakes to uncover requirements

In most software teams, strides are taken at the beginning of a cycle of work to gather as much data and information as possible from the customer to understand requirements as completely as possible. Nevertheless, it's not unheard of for a seemingly unimportant detail to be overlooked during this phase of the project, only to either become a blocking problem midway through development, or to go completely unnoticed and later be revealed as a key requirement whilst you're showcasing your work.

Use these situations as opportunities to figure out how you can improve next time: what information didn't you have that you wish you'd had? How could you have elicited that information from the customer? Could you have broken tasks down further to discover hidden requirements? Questions such as these will help your team improve with each new project, and ultimately you'll deliver better work and make your customers even happier.

One way to try to discover hidden requirements is to carry out research spikes. On a software team, this would typically involve one engineer dedicating a small but significant amount of time, such as half a day or a whole day, to investigating whether a potential solution is worth spending more time on.

It's a long enough period of time that some thorough research can be done, but short enough that, if it doesn't pan out, the loss of time isn't too much to bear. The researcher is also safe in the knowledge that, should the research lead nowhere, the team won't consider it a failure.

Using mistakes and mentoring to help teach new skills

Less experienced members of the team may struggle with

tasks other engineers find simple. As we've said, engineers at every level are constantly facing new challenges, and mistakes are bound to happen. However, when you have junior engineers working alongside senior engineers, the environment you're creating should allow juniors to feel safe enough to approach their more experienced peers for guidance. To take it even further, encouraging your senior engineers to take an active interest in mentoring is a great way to quickly upskill newer members of the team.

Using mistakes to analyse common problems and automate them away

Software engineers love to automate all the things, but there'll always be the occasional process that's still being performed manually and, no matter how often the process is performed, the more convoluted it is, the more likely it is that a crucial step is overlooked, leading to a failure.

Back in the day, before the advent of source control, something as fundamental as deploying changes to a production environment was a manual process, and involved massive amounts of risk. If the deploy broke anything on production, you had to cross your fingers and hope that someone on the team had a historical copy of the offending file. That problem was solved with a combination of solutions such as Git and Jenkins, which give us the ability to easily deploy and move software through various testing environments all the way to a production environment at the touch of a button. If anything is broken, we can then easily roll the latest changes back.

Within your organisation, there are likely several

risky and complex processes that are causing your team frustration. By allowing your team to identify and discuss these problems, you're giving them the ability to work together to find a solution that reduces the risk and transforms the process from one that causes frustration to one that is almost mundane.

Mistakes and failures are not something to be feared, in fact, celebrating them is perhaps more appropriate. That statement sounds a little ridiculous but, when you consider how much a failure can teach you about the work you're doing, the way you're doing it and how you can help others do it, there's too much valuable knowledge to be garnered from a mistake to set about reprimanding someone for making it.

by Scott Mason

CHAPTER 11
CLIENT SHOWCASES

At Made Tech we host regular client showcases, this is an opportunity to sit down with the client to discuss how the iteration and the project as a whole are progressing.

Who should be involved with a showcase?

The most important people to be involved in a showcase are the developers working on the iteration, the key stakeholders on the clients side. A showcase cannot happen without these people. Additionally, any members of the client's business whose lives will be improved by the work carried out ought to be involved. For example, a customer service representative or an e-commerce manager. These people will have valuable, on the ground, insights into existing problems it should solve and potential challenges the work may introduce before its too late.

An alternative showcase can be one made internally, to educate other teams in your organisation on things you've learned, the project you've been working on, any reusable software you've built and practices you'd like others to adopt. It's important to do this formally as a showcase, because it allows people the opportunity to comment and give feedback. You don't get this kind of honest technical feedback from clients, so it can be more than a chance to share, it can be invaluable peer review.

Why do good software teams showcase?

A showcase is a prime time to get your work in front of all key stakeholders to demonstrate how your work is progressing, and how this impacts the project and their business. It is extremely important to have these regularly, to ensure client and developer expectations are kept in sync. Without this regular contact point, delivered work may fall short in some areas and over-deliver in other areas, both of which are a waste of developer time and the clients resources. By instead ensuring you and your client are on the same page, everybody will be happy with the delivered iteration, and any potential problems will surface before it's too late, again saving time and money.

Additionally, by involving people in the showcase who will actually personally benefit from the work being done, this gives you an opportunity to demonstrate and teach processes and functionality to these end users. We notice this in particular when building new tools for businesses. Overall it reduces the time spent up-skilling these people later on, and gives them a good opportunity to recommend improvements.

Furthermore, a showcase is an excellent forum to openly discuss any feedback the client may have on the past iteration and the shape of the project in general, and to line up the goals of the next iteration if relevant.

We've found it useful to give internal showcases to people outside of the project team, so that we can update everyone across the company on what the team have achieved,, what they've learned, any practices the wider team should adopt or avoid, and any technical achievements that could be co-op'd into other projects.

Introducing better showcases into your team

Things which are important to consider when introducing showcases in a project are structure and frequency. Enforcing good structure in your showcases will ensure the time is well spent for all parties. Make sure the first and most important part of the showcase is demonstrating what you've been up to, discussing any problems you faced and solved, any problems you still have, and not allowing interruptions or tangents to take place until the end. The benefit of this is clients have time to consider, condense and prioritise feedback, and those leading the showcase are able to make all of their points undistracted.

Additionally, showcases provide a personal growth opportunity for developers. We believe showcases should be led by developers. This puts a certain amount of pressure on them, but we think it's beneficial pressure to have. This is because they are the people with the best understanding of the work, the people who can most easily gauge and accept feedback and the people who will have to carry out the rest of the work. Additionally, it encourages their best work as they know they will have to stand up and be accountable for it in front of clients. We've found this kind of growth is often best achieved by pushing people in at the deep end and providing them with a float, rather than wading them in gently. This sink or swim approach sounds brutal, but encourages autonomy and personal confidence in the individual.

Preparation

During an iteration we find it useful to keep note of all the wins and challenges we've had, on top of the tasks we've completed. This enables us to easily prepare a run down of the iteration. These run down documents then get stored inside the project, similar to a changelog to provide a contextual history of a project.

After the run down has been prepared it is often valuable to run through it with other members of the project team to ensure smooth delivery, and catch any shortcomings, complexity, and omissions. This is particularly important when finishing an iteration where it is important to put your best foot forward and deliver a slick demo.

Additionally, a practiced showcase enables you to efficiently time-box the demonstration, as an ideal showcase lasts a maximum of 10-15 minutes. If you find your showcases are longer than this, consider shortening your iteration times and focusing on smaller chunks of work. Keeping it concise also means you also allow time for questions, feedback, and thoughtful discussions about the work presented.

Mid point showcases

A mid point showcase is an opportunity to present work in

progress and ensure the client's expectations are being met before the end of the iteration, where it may be too late to change, and certainly more costly. Having frequent showcases allows them more opportunity to give feedback and have more of a say in the way a feature is developed. Developers may also discover areas of improvement over the original specification of the feature, having built and used it. Features are often not built exactly to specification; UX and UI changes are made throughout the build and, as web professionals, we're well placed to make this kind of feedback to our clients.

Secondly, as this is work in progress, it's important you make this clear to the client beforehand, so they're confident you'll be able to work on the fine details together, and focus on whether the high priority, wider feature is being completed correctly. For example, frontend tweaks can be made, but the backend logic is coming together as they wanted. If you do receive any feedback, it is important to keep it focused on the demonstrated functionality, and not inflate the scope of the iteration, and to do your best to only capture top level information as more detailed discussions should be made with the client when you come to address it. You want enough to be able to triage it later, but not so much that the showcase goes on too long or anybody loses focus.

It's also an excellent opportunity to set expectations early if you feel you won't complete the piece of work by the end of the iteration, and give clear honest reasons behind this, for example if a "quick win" task which we didn't expect to take long ended up taking a day. This will prevent the team from having to break bad news at the end of the iteration when work is incomplete, when the client was expecting fully featured work. Being honest about these problems builds a better relationship with the client and ensures they understand that you faced an unforeseen problem, and not that the team were slacking off. It's positive to build this relationship of trust, and that comes from openness.

Additionally, bringing up adversity early gives the client an opportunity to back out early rather than wasting further time. For example, if the team was to discover the work would take twice as long as expected, the client should have an opportunity to re-evaluate their business priorities if they have other high priority features that may now be considered more valuable. Furthermore in this situation they may want to park the other work if they were depending on the time staying fixed, as they have other time sensitive work upcoming.

End of iteration showcases

The primary purpose of the end of iteration showcase is for the team to present all the work they've agreed to deliver, excluding any work previously removed from the scope of the iteration, which should have happened at the mid point showcase. Not to mention, a perfect time to show off.

During the showcase you should make a point to highlight unseen wins, for example shining a light on complexity within the iteration where it existed. This builds your client's confidence in your teams ability to deliver technical work and solve problems. Also point out areas where the team have gone above and beyond to deliver unexpected value. You can often find easy opportunities to improve a feature by chance, that is a quick win to implement, and highlighting these value adds delights the client. This promotes a more trusting "Adult to Adult" relationship. It will be beneficial to the ongoing project if you are seen as partners rather than contractors.

If you've taken the time to implement additional functionality to help an end user, which you believe will save the client time and money in the long run, you should take the time to point these out as well.

Although ideally the work your team has delivered will be as expected by the client, often additional requirements fall out of new features, which should be captured at the end of your showcase. If they are minor tweaks, these new requirements should be stored in your project backlog and then prioritised by the client. However you will sometimes begin to pad out the next iteration off the back of a final showcase.

Post Showcase

The time after a showcase, before the next iteration begins, is a good chance to reflect on the iteration. It's worth congratulating everybody on a job well done by highlighting things individuals, and the team as a whole, did well, which you'd like to see happen more. You should also take the time to evaluate areas of the delivery and development of the iteration which didn't go so well, which should be learned from for all future iterations. To name a few examples, if the iteration was slowed by interactions with a third party which could have been mitigated beforehand by starting conversations earlier, if you began work before the design was finalised, or if you waited too long to get code into a production environment. These are all lessons we've learned from over the years.

Furthermore, when celebrating triumphs and learning from shortcomings, it is important to share this with your wider organisation. For example, if you've solved a recurring or complex technical problem and produced a reusable solution which other teams could use, or discovered a flaw in a company process which you'd like to evolve together. Keeping these learnings to yourself can cause fragmentation in the knowledge of different teams, and prevent you from raising everybody up together.

To reiterate, hosting frequent structured showcases is an excellent way to keep lines of communication open, and ensure client expectations always meet your own. Having developers run these makes them accountable, promotes autonomy, and boosts confidence. You should use them to share your work, capture constructive feedback, and backlog new requirements.

Don't be timid when you encounter adversity, and involve the customer when you do. This ensures they are able to make informed, timely business decisions. After your showcase learn from your strides, and miss-steps, and take the time to spread this knowledge amongst the wider organisation.

Client Showcases

A perfect showcase involves a minimal number of people for brevity, but these need to be the right people. You should invite key stakeholders along, like the project manager, as well as a relevant end user. Most importantly keep your client happy, and keep the work flowing!

by Seb Ashton & Richard Foster

CHAPTER 12

RECRUITMENT

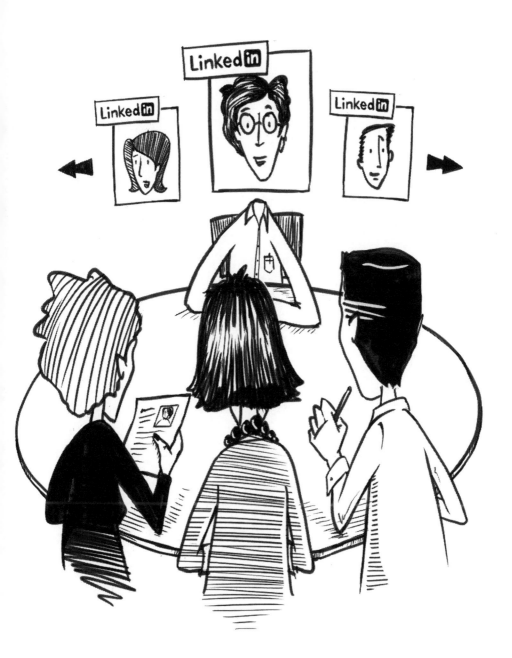

Recruiting the right group of people is one of the most important parts of building a top software delivery team. In this article, we take a look at some things you should consider whilst recruiting, and a few things that you should try to avoid.

Create a cohesive culture

A key component of building an effective software delivery team is creating a cohesive culture. A cohesive culture is achieved when a team feels empowered to participate, can collaborate effectively and gets recognition for its successes. To achieve this you need the right leadership, the right mix of experience, and people with character traits that encourage cohesion.

When recruiting, you should be thinking about how to achieve a cohesive culture. Often people recruit with specific technical skills in mind, but we've found that it's just as important to consider softer skills such as:

- Is this person a team player?

- Are they able to communicate effectively?

- Do they take responsibility or blame others?

- Do they have a positive outlook?

Although there isn't a 'one size fits all' approach to creating a cohesive culture, there are certainly signs that you can look out for during an interview process and, when you see them, question whether the candidate is somebody who will help encourage cohesion, or fight against it.

Don't hire rockstars, ninjas or self-proclaimed superstars

Everybody wants to hire incredibly talented people, but never hire anyone who considers themselves a 'rockstar' engineer. It's a sign of arrogance and an inflated ego, and they're a sure fire way to create a divided team. Of course, you want exceptional people on your team, just make sure they're grounded and able to put their skills to good use, improving the team.

Leverage your network

It's nearly always better to recruit through your existing network. Either through people you have worked with previously, or through contacts your team have within the industry.

Your team should understand the needs of the organisation and what it's like to work there. Their relationship with a candidate will mean they already know a lot more than can be discovered during an interview process.

These kind of network referrals are the best indication you'll get as to whether or not a candidate will be successful, so favour them over other recruitment sources.

Referral bonuses

It has become common for organisations to offer incentives to staff to help encourage recruitment referrals. In our experience, awesome people will automatically want to bring their most talented friends and acquaintances along. Offering incentives can help and may result in a few additional hires, but it's questionable as to whether carrot and stick motivation ultimately leads to stronger teams.

Our advice would be to focus on building a great culture, that your team are proud of, and their network of acquaintances will be eager to join. You can still thank people for referrals but, hopefully, you'll find that by flipping the motivation model from extrinsic to intrinsic, you'll end up in a happier place.

Strive for diversity

It's no secret that many software teams struggle with diversity. While there are some factors limiting progress, diversity is something that needs to be taken into account when recruiting. There are steps that you can take, such as:

- Helping people to reduce unconscious bias

- Capturing and reviewing data that highlights diversity challenges within your organisation

- Scrutinising job advertisements and internal practices to ensure they don't unintentionally discourage certain demographics.

We've made significant progress in recent years, but our industry has a long way to go in terms of diversity, and there's a lot we can do to create an environment that is welcoming of people from any walk of life. Bear this in mind when recruiting!

Keep it interesting, increase retention

One of the challenges you'll face after you've recruited some good people is keeping them around. If they are talented and based in a decent location, then they are likely to have many opportunities open to them.

It's common to see companies offer perks and incentives to help encourage employees to stick around. In our experience, the most important factor is ensuring they can keep on learning, improving and getting better. This means having work that is challenging, and is going to push them to improve every week. If this dries up and day-to-day becomes mundane, you'll often find people won't stick around.

Above-market salaries

Where possible, you should look to take money off the table

and pay above industry wages. This often helps to attract a higher calibre of individual (providing you're recruiting well!) and shows your team that you value them.

This approach is particularly relevant in fields which are highly leveraged and where software delivery is generating a good ROI. When this is the case, it can make sense to pay well above market rates and get above-average performers, as it can be a win for the organisation and a win for the employee.

Of course, this approach is dependent on an organisation being in a very strong and stable financial position, which tends to limit the number of organisations that can do this.

Don't use contractors

The software industry has a large number of people who work on a contract basis. In our experience, it's inadvisable to build software teams comprised primarily of contractors.

We have found the most efficient teams to be those who have worked together for extended periods of time. This typically means full-time staff. We tend to find contract staff can take a short-term view, and this can mean your delivery teams are in a constant state of flux.

When you have to use contractors, try to use them sparingly. We've seen technology teams 100+ strong, comprised of over 90% contractors and struggling to deliver. We would advise keeping contractor levels to a minimum at all times.

Firing underperformers

It's human nature to avoid making difficult decisions. Nobody wants to be fired or to have to tell someone that they no longer have a job. However, when faced with this scenario, it's vital that you act quickly and let them go as soon as possible.

It's a sad truth that many organisations end up carrying underperforming team members for years. This can have a big impact on morale and wider team performance, so it's important that the situation is dealt with.

Embrace juniors

If you're hiring junior team members, it's important that you factor in some of the challenges that this can bring. Juniors often require significantly more support than expected, which can impede the team and impact ability to ship quickly.

Sometimes you need to slow down in order to speed up, and we think this is particularly relevant when onboarding junior members into a team.

Make sure your environment provides plenty of support for juniors and opportunities to learn. Things like mentors, pair programming, regular code dojos or code katas can all help, and over time the level of support and guidance required should drop significantly.

Colocate or remote

Nowadays it's common to see companies offering remote roles. We see some significant benefits to this, such as a much wider talent pool, ability to get more focused time and a better work-life balance. However, there are trade offs. One example is that it can be far more difficult to achieve a cohesive culture team when you've got people working remotely.

We've found a good balance is to have people working remotely part-time, so maybe two or three days per week. This has given us some of the benefits of remote working, with some of the upsides of colocation and has worked well.

Onboard effectively

The first few weeks with a new hire is a crucial time. They are going to decide during those weeks whether the company is actually a good fit and whether they have made the right choice.

Ensure you set aside ample time to onboard new starters properly. Make them feel welcome and help them to get to know the team and understand how things work. Set very clear objectives, so they know what they are working towards and what criteria you've got for reviewing their performance during their probation period. Talk with them regularly and provide them with lots of encouragement and direction around areas they are doing well and could be doing better.

Retrospecting the interview process

As with any process, it's important to frequently assess performance and find ways to do things better. Recruitment is no different. Set aside time to talk to candidates about the recruitment process, to find out what has worked well and not so well for them.

We've explored running facilitated retrospectives with candidates we've employed and rejected. This has helped us understand what the next evolution of an interview process might look like and steps we would need to take to get there.

Recruiting a strong software delivery team is tough. It requires a huge amount of effort, starting with finding the right people, then convincing them to join and moulding them into a cohesive team that works well together. If you can achieve this, then you've done extremely well, and you are well on your way to building a high-performance software team.

You'll find that once you've got the first batch of great people onboard, it should start to get easier. Talented and motivated individuals tend to attract other talented and motivated individuals. With strong management, your team should continue to grow and improve for years to come.

by Rory MacDonald

Part 3: Empowerment

In this section, we look at a number of techniques that you can employ to increase the levels of empowerment in your team.

Teams with higher levels of empowerment often show increased levels of satisfaction, and subsequently deliver higher performance. Allowing people the freedom to structure their workload and workday can be a great first step to empowerment.

From here, explore a workflow whereby you express higher level problems or goals to the team, and then have the team themselves work to identify the solutions, and the best way to implement and deliver them.

With empowerment, it's also important to balance accountability. An empowered team who are tasked with solving higher level problems also need to have an appropriate level of accountability for delivering these solutions.

As an added bonus to great empowerment, more empowered and autonomous delivery teams can reduce reliance on the management tier of the organisation, allowing a greater ability to scale engineering efforts.

CHAPTER 13
CREATING ENVIRONMENTS FOR SAFE DEPLOYMENT

Developers should be allowed to deploy at any time. Many find this a scary prospect since it makes traditional release management and QA very hard. We have found that empowering developers to own the responsibility of deployment allows you to ship software much faster whilst maintaining or even improving the safety of releasing changes when compared to more traditional processes.

As part of our mission to improve software delivery in every organisation we seek to bring our customers on a journey from deploying once a quarter to a few times a day.

What do we mean by deploying safely at any time?

Anyone who introduces a new feature, makes an improvement or fixes a bug should be allowed to push that change into production and should take responsibility for that change. The engineer will not only make a change to the code but deploy it, ensure that it functions as expected in production and even be in touch with the stakeholders of the feature whether they be customers or colleagues to announce the changes. Should anything go wrong, they are responsible for fixing it.

There are many safe guards that accompany a continuous deployment practice. We for example have a production-like environment that we test against before putting changes live. We also have automated testing and code reviews where other engineers are asked to review work before it's allow to be released.

Why should everyone deploy their own changes?

Before going into the details of explaining how to create a safe environment it's probably best we answer the "why" first.

The biggest benefit when empowering teams to deploy more often is that change becomes less risky. By making more frequent changes they will naturally be smaller. If our deployments are smaller they will be easier to test and easier to fix in the case of any issues. Deployments should become mundane.

Over time your team will become better at testing their own changes and fixing issues when they arise. When a developer releases a change they will learn to become responsible for testing and monitoring it. This creates a proactive culture where developers can quickly react to problems often allowing them to spot defects before many users encounter them.

Releasing more often also means changes get into the hands of your users faster. Removing overheads such as QA processes means that we can make changes quickly, reacting to market changes and the metrics we collect.

Not only do the business and customers benefit from more frequent releases but we've found empowered developers are happier developers. By being responsible for a change, from start to finish, developers will feel a sense of pride and ownership over their work. We've found more traditional release strategies lead to developers passing responsibility onto QA or the deployment teams, simply throwing their work over the fence. When developers own their changes, they will put care into their work.

One common argument that may come up is that developers will be swapping depth of knowledge in a particular field for breadth which spans many fields. While this is a reasonable concern we have found that this is not as drastic as it may seem and almost always engineers prefer the responsibility of owning the whole problem.

How do you provide a safe deployment environment?

From our experiences we have found the following 6 steps to greatly improve the way in which software is deployed. These can be expanded on but having these in place will greatly benefit your releases.

- Create a safe environment where it is ok to fail

- Make deployments easier by automating them

- Ensure the deployment pipeline is fast

- Deploy to a production-like environment for testing before going live

- Get used to deploying small changes

- Tell everyone about your deployments when they happen

- Set up monitoring so you know when you deploy a breaking change

- Use blue green deployments so rolling back is easy

We'll now briefly go into each one of these subjects although each could, and in some cases do, have entire blog posts about them.

Encourage a culture where it is ok to fail

In order to benefit from deploying faster, you first need a culture where failure is ok. It is rare in software engineering that changes are perfect first time round. Optimising for fixing failures quickly provides more value than getting things right the first time round. This is sometimes called optimising for MTTR (Mean Time To Repair) rather than MTBF (Mean Time Between Failures).

Failure can often lead to blame. Instead of making failure a negative situation everyone in your team should understand that failure happens and is in fact a great opportunity to learn from and develop. When failure happens, the team should stand together, jump on the problem as a team and then discuss what happened afterwards with the aim of improving things for the future.

When you have a friendly environment for people to work in, they will produce better work. Don't punish failure, reward recovery.

Make deployments easier by automating them

Humans aren't great at repeating processes, and let's face it, repeating yourself can be boring too. A typical deployment will include building, testing and releasing the software to the public. Each of these steps are themselves made up of a series of smaller steps.

Use scripts for each step in your pipeline so each step can be executed with one command. You can use services like Travis CI, Circle CI and Codeship, or self-hosted solutions like Jenkins to run scripts automatically for you. For example when a new change has been peer reviewed and accepted by merging the change into the main codebase, code hosting platforms like GitHub can automatically trigger your build and testing scripts for you.

Deployment scripts can be triggered manually or automatically when the previous steps are completed. Even if an engineer has to click a button to put a change live, that's a lot less error prone than running scripts, or a sequence of commands manually.

Ensure the deployment pipeline is fast

When a problem occurs in production, you'll want to fix it as quick as you can. Once diagnosis of the problem has occurred, and a fix applied locally, you'll want to ship that change out fast. In order to do this your pipeline needs to be quick too. Even larger projects should only be taking 10-20 minutes to go through the pipeline with the ideal speed being much lower than that.

Being able to react fast can often mean rather than needing to roll back, you can in fact roll forward. In reality this means rather than removing a new feature when you find an issue you can instead fix it quickly. Of course, if it's a more serious problem, rolling back or disabling the feature would most likely be the correct course of action.

Deploy to a production-like environment for testing before going live

Before putting a change live that has only been run on an developer or two's laptop, you'll want an environment that you can test it on that mimics production. Often local development configuration will use different settings and modes, particularly when it comes to what type of databases it uses and debugging settings. A change in these conditions like when an application moves from development to production can be a source of errors. You'll want a production-like setup in order to discover these errors before things go live.

In order to facilitate a production-like environment ideally everything from server setup, database configuration, data stored in the database should be nearly identical to production. One consideration with data is that you may want to copy data from production into your production-like environment but you'll want to replace customer emails with example ones otherwise you may end up sending emails to customers from your production-like environment.

Get used to deploying small changes

When deploys are kept small, to something like 100-200 lines of code or smaller, risk is limited. It's fairly obvious that when your changes only impact a smaller surface area of a system, when something goes wrong, there will be a smaller area to search within to find the problem.
Smaller changes will also mean that peer reviewing and testing are a quicker process. Again a smaller surface area is easier to look over, easier to test the various pathways through it.

To reduce risk, instead of deploying whole features, deploy tens of times before the feature is complete. You do not need to make the feature publicly accessible until the last release but by dark launching it into production you will be uncovering a lot of problems early, avoiding the big bang release and the problems that come with it.

Tell everyone about your deploys when they happen

If you have automated your deploys, you'll also be able to automate the broadcasting of this deploy. It is important to let everyone know about change when it happens so everyone can have a look at the new functionality, be alert and ready for when any issues occur, and also to celebrate yet another release.

You could consider automatically emailing the team and wider business when changes go live. If you use chat applications like Slack you could set up alerts within appropriate channels. You could even start emailing your customers automatically if you're brave.

Set up monitoring so you know when you deploy a breaking change

You need good monitoring in your application so that when an error occurs, or page load of a web application slows down, you are alerted to the problem. After any deploy to production, the developer who pushed it up should keep an eye on the monitoring to see if any defects had been introduced but should also be notified automatically of any such issues.

Since the nature of change does carry some risk the goal is to spot potential defects before the issue affects a greater number of people.

Tools such as NewRelic allow you to set up alerts when certain performance thresholds are exceeded along with notifying of errors that happen to applications.

Use blue green deployments so rolling back is easy

If you deploy frequently and monitor the system after each deploy, you should have a pretty clear picture on which deploy had adverse effects on the system. If you have a fast pipeline, you'll likely be able to roll forward if the issue isn't too great. But what if you do need to rollback?

Using blue green deployments is a safe way to deploy a new production. Essentially when you have a new release ready you deploy it to a new server rather than immediately replacing the old production server. You can then visit this version of the application, make sure it's okay, then point the domain name of production at the new server thereby switching web traffic over to the new version.

Blue green deployments have the benefit that if something goes wrong, you can point the domain back at the old version again in order to rollback. Of course it also gives you another opportunity to test your changes before showing them to the world.

Trust your teams

It all comes down to trust. Developers should be allowed to deploy at any time in most cases. We should learn to recover from failure fast, and learn all the lessons failure can teach us.

by Luke Morton & Emile Swarts

161

CHAPTER 14

GIVING TEAMS FREEDOM TO STRUCTURE THEIR OWN TIME

HAPPY PRODUCTIVE CHAP.

It can be scary to devolve a lot of managerial and planning responsibility to teams but we've found lots of positives in changing the way we approach time management. Allowing teams the ability to plan their workloads, holidays, working location and client engagement has resulted in a greater sense of ownership on projects.

As a result of these changes we've noticed:

- Better quality of work through sense of ownership

- Better value in engagements for our clients

- Better relationships with the clients

- A reduction in the overhead around planning for holidays, etc.

It's essential however that management are confident enough in their teams to place this trust in them.

Communicating with clients

Before a team is about to start development, having introductions with the client will prove beneficial during the development period.

Traditional approaches have been for there to be a project manager to act as the go between from developers to clients and vice versa. This has always added extra time into a project - usually time spent waiting on responses. This can lead to stop-start interruptions which normally result in developers downing tools, and starting other work to fill the gaps.

What harm is there in empowering the team to communicate directly with the client and enhance the relationship?

For starters it'll save a bunch of time. When a developer is unsure of something, rather than risking development time that will potentially need to be backtracked later, give the client a call or IM them to get faster feedback or clarification around the work. It's essential that the team and client can create a fast feedback cycle to reduce the potential for interruptions to the development process.

Developers will better understand client priorities if they're communicating directly, rather than being shielded unnecessarily from them. It helps that a team is conscious of these, so that they can make decisions that add better business value for the client.

When holding standups and meetings with clients the team should keep in mind what the client's level of technical understanding is and make sure not to just use lots of technical speak. If people walk away from a meeting not understanding what's happened then that's a big failing in the communication process. Potentially this can cause misunderstandings where clients and developers aren't on the same page.

Through identifying the client's priorities, and the constant communication, the team is well placed to shape the work for each iteration without outside guidance.

Establishing work process

Early on in building the engagement with the client, the intended work process should be discussed and explained to the client so that they'll be on the same page as the developers when they're introduced. Clients need to be sold on the advantages of devolving management to the team while also knowing they can reach out to others in the business if they need to.

One of the main advantages gained through this process is the ability for the team and client to plan short iterations that allow for showcases of the work throughout development. The team should be able to identify the priority for each iteration through this close relationship with the client and be able to depend on the client throughout iterations to provide feedback and guidance around any ambiguous areas.

On longer running engagements this should mean the stakeholder on the client side participates in the team's standup and is available via the communication formats outlined above throughout the day. It's important that developers can contact them quickly with any queries or concerns. This also helps foster a closer relationship between the client and the business.

Ideally showcases ought to be run by the development team, extra points for rotating chair duties, who should focus on the work that was defined as being part of the iteration following the last showcase. Any feedback that comes from this showcase should be part of the next iteration rather than being added to a backlog where possible. If feedback is left open you run the risk of it getting lost, the client feeling ignored, or the original issue becoming unusable and not providing any value to the client.

Establishing the business process

Clients are onboard with this new way of working. But is the team? Do they really have the freedom to do all they need to self-organise? Do they feel trusted?

We have a handbook that the entire world can see, and allows us to keep our processes repeatable and transparent.

The handbook outlines how the business expects individuals to organise things like holidays and remote work (to be discussed later on in more detail) so that the team can effectively shape their workload.

By making holidays and remote work visible to everyone via shared calendars, these decisions can be easily made by the team, and also allow the individual to make a quick judgement call on the viability of a request.

For example while we might let everyone know we want to take a week off or work from home, we only require our team mates to ok it.

Let team members communicate with one another

It's equally important for team members to be able to communicate amongst themselves without barriers. Where a team member is shouldn't increase friction in communicating with the rest of the team. Our office is spread over three floors, and people are often spread out over the entirety of it and others are working remotely. Team communication needs to work for all these scenarios. This is where tooling is important for it to be a success.

Day-to-day the team need to be able to attend standup no matter where they are. Them being out of the office shouldn't be a barrier to participation. After all, a client is going to call into these, so the team needs to too. Test out the various tools to see what works best for your team and clients and use this wherever possible.

Remote work

Lots of business are against remote work, as they're worried they can't see people working but it's important when switching to self-organising teams to trust your workers to do their jobs without being watched.

When working remotely it's key that team mates and the clients are unaffected, the individual assumes the responsibility or maintaining the everyday standard these people are accustomed to. This means both the quality of work and the actual process, you don't want to be calling your client from a noisy place where the communication will suffer.

We feel we've got the correct toolset to allow for the entire company to be remote on a given day. Recently we had to contend with constant construction noise next to the office and all worked elsewhere for a day or two with no impact to the clients, workload or our day-to-day process. One of the things we do to increase people's presence when out of the office is to drop a quick message into our chat when we're going to be away for a period of time like at lunch.

Holidays

Beyond what we've outlined above the main thing with holidays is ensuring that enough of the team is still available to maintain momentum. As the team is scheduling their own holiday, make sure you don't forget to let the client know too if there are any changes to the team. In some cases other developers can be brought in to cover.

Holiday time must be taken into consideration when planning iterations so that they can set realistic goals/targets.

On the flip side, it's as important that the client lets the team know if they'll be away on holiday. In these cases an alternative stakeholder should be introduced to the team who'll be a point of contact.

Hackdays & learning days

As with holidays, since these are usually at least a day in length, the client needs to be made aware of these well in advance and reminded the day before during standup.

These normally involve the whole company, so whoever organises them is conscious that the company as a whole needs quite a bit of advance notice, at least a month.

We try and balance the frequency of these days. While we see them as valuable to the company as a whole, we don't want clients to feel like they're constantly taking a back seat.

Dojos

These are often recurring hourly sessions that happen weekly. These are self organised each time and if no one has an idea we don't run them as they're encouraged, but not mandatory.

If there is one scheduled, anyone participating is conscious of their current work load, and will only take part if it's not going to affect any the work due to be showcased. We also try to avoid scheduling client interactions when these are taking place to encourage maximum option to participate across all teams.

Knowledge sharing

It's essential to foster knowledge sharing as a cultural norm when enabling teams to self-organise. When people go on holiday, are ill or otherwise unavailable the team need to be able to keep functioning. To promote this we encourage frequent pairing throughout the company.

The constant switching of roles during pairing greatly facilitates technical, domain, and business knowledge to be quickly shared between teammates. It's also a great way to bring a new team member up-to-speed with an ongoing engagement.

Before a team member goes on holiday they should be sure to handover anything that only they have had sight of, although try not to let that happen. If this information isn't recent it's worth looking at how communication is working across the team.

On the client side, it can be difficult to fully envision and grasp the use cases without going on site and working alongside the end users and stakeholders to understand their goals. Teams should feel empowered and encouraged to go to the client or bring them into the office to facilitate this transfer of knowledge. At the end of the day our clients know their business better than we do and that value should be leveraged.

Testing and phasing of processes

Depending on your business, introducing self-organising teams might be quite a drastic, big change to the business. There is no harm in trialling the introduction of this to a single team to begin with.

We tested this process with a single team, giving full visibility, control over holidays, scheduling iterations etc. to see how effectively it worked. This allowed us to make changes to the process, building confidence in it, before rolling it out across the company.

With processes that have been rolled out company wide, we still experiment and make changes. We're never afraid to change processes if we think they can be better. Don't be against something until you've tried it!

Management

Devolving this power to teams doesn't mean that management can't be there to assist and guide teams. There is still a lot of valuable knowledge and insight that the teams can benefit from.

With the teams directly communicating with clients, it's still important for them to know the long term roadmap of work. It's just nice to know so there are fewer surprises for developers day-to-day.

If a manager sees that a team is struggling, then this is a good time to assist, not taking control, but offering guidance on how to proceed and communicating with the client if need be.

Hopefully the points we've covered will help you apply this to your teams. We've learned it's essential to be open to change, realising what works for you and what doesn't will be an important part of forming your own processes and norms around self-organising.

We've found these to be a good basis for Made Tech but don't feel that any of these are hard rules. As part of empowering your teams, allow them a say in shaping how best to find what works for them.

by Ryan MacGillivray & David Winter

CHAPTER 15
DISMANTLING SILOS

A silo exists in an organisation when one group within the organisation has differing goals to another. In most organisations there are groups of people that, usually, have an objective to fulfil by an agreed upon date. For example, the Sales team is set a mandate to increase the number of customers of the company by 10% every month, whereas the Support team has internal performance goals, and one of them is to deliver support within a fixed budget.

These teams have the freedom to innovate to achieve their goals. The Sales team choose to slash the price of their product, and immediately it is flying off the shelves; the Sales team are celebrating! The Support team however are now under pressure, and cannot offer a quality service to all their new customers without new members of staff. Due to the product's newly discounted price tag, the company cannot afford this extra operational cost.

Before long, the company gets a reputation for poor customer support. These two silos, sales and support, have potentially compromised the future of the enterprise.

What happened here is that this organisation had failed to see the broader picture. Although this example is fictitious, it is easy to imagine happening in the real world.

Software teams

At Made Tech, we commonly encounter silos within our client organisations, so one of our top priorities on a new engagement is the alignment of our customer's goals. Cutting through these silos is critical to avoiding scenarios like the one discussed above, and to ensure that our software delivers the greatest value to the whole business.

In situations where our point of contact has a silo-goal, failure to identify this quickly means software can be designed and delivered which does not benefit the wider company aims. Aside from making it difficult to deliver simple solutions for the organisation in the future, this can also have an impact on working relationships.

Goal misalignments are usually unintentional, so it is important to mitigate these behaviours with activities designed to aid delivering great solutions for the whole business.

Communicating with Stakeholders

To understand an organisation's aims in detail, gathering a list of stakeholders and understanding their goals and how they fit into the bigger picture is often useful. One technique that we have found works very well is the use of regular client showcases. These showcases ensure that the parties concerned with the delivery of solutions are kept involved in the evolution of the plan, and feel a sense of ownership of the direction in which the project is going.

Communicating with Specialists

A common way teams organise themselves is to group individuals according to their specialisms. Within the tech world, this has resulted in teams such as Backend, Frontend and QA, each of which have different yardsticks by which to measure success, and are therefore at risk not communicating effectively with other departments.

A traditional silo is that of an IT department, viewed

as a cost centre. Meanwhile, profit-building software delivery teams are depending on this IT Department for both hardware and software. It is not in the best interest of a company attempting to deploy a new software artefact to production, to be held up by another department that holds the keys.

Uncovering hidden goals

Hidden goals are those goals which are usually found within silos and not shared with the broader business. Inadequate communication is often the cause for these hidden goals, and although it is not reasonable to expect them to all be discovered early on in the development process, it is worth actively seeking them out.

We have found that practising Continuous Delivery is a useful tool for uncovering such goals, given that it allows for a frequent and detailed feedback loop with stakeholders. We can showcase potential solutions regularly, giving stakeholers an effective forum to guide the direction of the project.

Despite this, goals can remain hidden even after showcases. When stakeholders offer feedback on your solution, that feedback may be the product of a hidden goal. It is therefore important to test assumptions about why these changes are being made. Be sure to ask questions about any feedback, even if the answer appears obvious.

Detecting silos

Observation is key to discovering silos, and in most companies, it isn't immediately obvious where they are. To give you a feel for what type of activities are indicative of silos we have compiled a list from the trenches to help you in your endeavours.

Communication go-betweens

Communication go-betweens operating as a proxy between engineering and customers, can lead to situations where software engineers are unable to get meaningful feedback on the solutions that they are delivering. Useful and accurate feedback is critical to shipping well-built and well-designed software.

Prescribed solutions

Controlling every detail of a solution in a top-down fashion removes freedom from software delivery teams. Lack of liberty makes it less desirable or necessary for cross-functional teams to emerge (through interdepartmental collaboration). Moreover, this freedom is key to the production of truly innovative and simple solutions. Managers should not need to be involved in every single minutia of a solution, only that the software delivery teams are solving the most pressing strategic issues.

Passing the buck

When no department can deal with an unexpected critical issue and instead passes the buck to another, it can indicate that no team or individual holds true accountability for resolving that issue. The underlying problem is that it shows that people are not aligned with the goals of the company itself. This conflict with the business indicates that those departments passing the buck have formed a silo against the organisation itself.

Lack of robust goal setting

How the evaluation of each team's performance is measured can be a reliable indicator of a silo. In the most extreme case, every department has a balance sheet. This financially-led approach can promote unhealthy internal competition and discourage collaboration between teams. The symptom here is that the goals of two organisational units are at odds with each other. This is compounded if there is no clear process available to staff, through which they can resolve their differences.

Organisational separation

Allocating departmental budgets, or in extreme cases, spinning out separately registered companies, can introduce difficult to solve organisational impediments that make it difficult to deliver on company goals. Collaborating across balance sheets becomes politically risky, and can result in the onset of "officially political cultures".

Competitive individual KPIs

When the performance evaluation of individuals prevents or discourages collaboration and knowledge-sharing there is no incentive to behave strategically. This friction can create problems internally for a single department just as much as cross-departmentally. For example, engineers may decide it is not in their best interest interest to behave collaboratively, potentially reducing the quality and speed of delivery of solutions.

Hiring

The hiring policy is a good indicator of silos within departments; departments can fight for expansion which can prevent hires elsewhere in critical areas of the business. Hiring without a clear and mutually agreed reason in mind could lead to hiring in the wrong places or for the wrong reasons. Many companies encourage departments to compete over recruiting budgets, but this doesn't solve real business problems. The interview process itself might highlight the competition between teams, such as when other teams are unaware of the recruitment but are still expected to work with the new hire.

How to break down silo mentality

Now that you have a better understanding of how to spot a

silo, it's possible to begin breaking them down by doing the following:

- Establish shared goals to ensure that departmental goals have organisational alignment.

- Ensure the organisation has high-level goals, above all departments to which departmental goals help meet.

- Ensure organisational goals are directly related to the vision.

-

Once this framework is in place, it becomes trivial for anyone within an organisation to set highly aligned personal, project, or product goals that directly impact the business achieving its targets.

It is important to get departments to speak to each other on important matters, such as how they will attain their goals collaboratively. For example, a digital design department should meet regularly with a software engineering department to determine how they will ship an online software product together.

Departments should not communicate solely through hierarchies; a junior software engineer could and should be in direct contact with designers.

As this evolves, it becomes clearer that it is more efficient to have departments working alongside each other to deliver a product. When people with different skillsets need to collaborate with the same goal, they should attend the same meetings, be aware of the same problems, and have a clear sense of shared direction and purpose.

Requiring formality or involving convoluted chains of command at this stage will only hinder collaboration. At this point, management shifts to a broader view of the company rather than micromanaging all daily details. Instead, the freedom granted to the team allows them to deliver continuously and ship products more quickly. Tighter collaboration between skillsets leads to better product quality thanks to a better understanding of the issues. Formal long meetings can be a symptom of having too much bureaucracy around collaboration, which can make it less desirable for employees to break down silos.

The really innovative companies are creating shared offices where teams with diverse skillsets (potentially cross-departmental) can collaborate. A psychological silo can manifest itself into a physical one with real walls and closed spaces inside the company. An analysis on how the office space is laid out can help to uncover potential silos.

Leaders should encourage everybody to work with anybody to solve company problems. Employees should be able to move freely to another team if needed for the current objectives, and the decision to attend a meeting should be made by anyone who believes it will achieve progress towards the higher company goals.

Silos create organisational bottlenecks. In any organisation, this can feel like arbitrary red tape, slowing progress for no real reason. For software teams, an individual having exclusive domain knowledge means the team's ability to develop and release software is hampered when said individual is unavailable. Look for ways to ensure such knowledge is shared amongst the whole team by making everyone aware of the goals your organisation has, and the role the software they're building plays in pursuit of those goals.

by Craig Bass, Luke Benellick and Alex Minette

About Made Tech

Made Tech are public sector technology delivery experts. We provide Digital, Data and Technology services across the UK market.

We help public sector leaders to modernise legacy applications and working practices, accelerate digital service delivery, drive smarter decisions with data and enable improved technology skills within teams.

Founded in 2012, we grew by helping startups to build products fast using lean and agile principles. Since 2016, we have been helping public sector organisations to adopt these skills, capabilities and ways of working to deliver better outcomes for citizens.

Find us at www.madetech.com

Printed in Great Britain
by Amazon

76053970R00104